Praise for *Redeeming Pleasure*

"Rarely does a book combine theological insight with practical wisdom the way *Redeeming Pleasure* does. With wit, wisdom, humor, and uncommon clarity, Jeremy helps us see that our hunger for pleasure is a legitimate, though often misdirected, part of our being made in God's image. And he reveals how it is often false, though commonly held, theological assumptions that get Christians off track. This is a book that has the power to revolutionize the way you think and beautifully transform the way you live. It is simply a MUST read!"

Dr. Gregory Boyd

Teaching Pastor, Woodland Hills Church, and Author and Coauthor of 20 books, including *The Myth of a Christian Nation*, *Letters from a Skeptic*, and *Repenting of Religion*

"In a culture of pleasure seekers, Jeremy Jernigan offers a counter-cultural yet life-giving perspective that will inspire, challenge, and free you deep in your soul."

Gene Appel

Senior Pastor of Eastside Christian Church

"Jeremy Jernigan is an important and much needed refreshing voice today. Whether through his writings or teachings, his insights on the scriptures inspire me to step fully into the kingdom life Jesus taught about. *Redeeming Pleasure* goes after the search we all hold so dear and clearly points us to the more fuller and expansive life Jesus promises. Such an incredible read!"

Teaching Pastor at V

"I think Christians have struggled for years with the subject of pleasure—good and bad. I grew up around Christians who never seemed to think pleasurable things were from God or even okay to pursue. I'm so excited that my friend Jeremy Jernigan has decided to tackle this tough conversation. He's an incredibly thoughtful and intelligent leader who is pastoring his church so well. I really believe *Redeeming Pleasure* will help many believers live more pleasurable lives because pleasure and joy come from God!"

Tyler Reagin

Executive Director for Catalyst

"Following Jesus and finding pleasure are often presented as mutually exclusive. You can have one or the other, but you can't have them both. Jeremy is addressing a subject that we desperately need to give our attention to as Christians living in an increasingly pleasure-obsessed culture. Jeremy helps us see how following Jesus and finding pleasure are related, because when you follow Jesus you will find true and lasting pleasure."

Kyle Idleman

Teaching Pastor at Southeast Christian Church
and Author of *Not A Fan*

"For those who think the Christian life should be all business and no pleasure, or for those whose self-serving pursuits of pleasure have left them feeling empty, *Redeeming Pleasure* is a must-read. Jeremy Jernigan paints a helpful picture of the goodness of God-given pleasure and what healthy habits of 'Christian hedonism' look like in a Jesus-honoring life."

Brett McCracken

Author of *Hipster Christianity* and *Gray Matters*

"Recently an Orthodox archbishop was asked if he had a message for the evangelical church in America. He instantly replied, 'Your moralism is killing you.' I believe the archbishop is right, which is why Jeremy Jernigan's *Redeeming Pleasure* is so timely and important. The God revealed in Christ is not a 'big policeman in the sky' glowering at humanity in constant disapproval. The God whom Jesus called Father is the author of pleasure, and He invites us to drink deeply from His river of delights. Jeremy provides us with a thoughtful and well-written exploration of divine delight."

Brian Zahnd

Lead Pastor of Word of Life Church
and Author of *A Farewell to Mars*

"For those of us who want to live life to the fullest, *Redeeming Pleasure* shows us how, and in ways we might never expect. Full of wisdom, humor, and honesty, I'm happy to recommend Jeremy Jernigan as someone well worth paying attention to."

Bruxy Cavey

Teaching Pastor at The Meeting House
and Author of the Bestseller *The End of Religion*

"In a culture crumbling from personal indulgence and pleasure overload, Jeremy Jernigan issues a prophet's corrective—not the denial of pleasure nor its simple indulgence, but a full-blown redemption of sex, work, and other God-given gifts. *Redeeming Pleasure* is a pleasure to read."

Tim Lucas

Lead Pastor of Liquid Church
and Author of *You Married the Wrong Person*

"It is normal to desire a life that has meaning and purpose, but when someone suggests pursuing pleasure, we are inclined to think of sinful acts or self-indulgence. Jeremy Jernigan challenges that traditional line of reasoning and casts a new light on what God desires for his children. He even takes on some controversial contemporary issues and the consequences of making rash judgments. *Redeeming Pleasure* will make you rethink some of your assumptions and show you how to blend biblical teachings about sacrificial living and self-denial with the concept of personal fulfillment within the grace of God."

Dr. John Derry

President of Hope International University

"We would all agree that our culture seems to get more and more off track, but Jeremy has hit the nail on the head with what ails us. Our relentless chase for fulfillment leads us down the broken road of pleasure gone haywire. *Redeeming Pleasure* is not only a great read but a must-read if we want to align ourselves with God's goodness and His gift of pleasure."

Rick Rusaw

Senior Minister of LifeBridge Church
and Author of *The Externally Focused Life*

"Jeremy Jernigan's *Redeeming Pleasure* is a call to Christian 'Epicureanism' and a 'liberating' read. It reminds one of the rabbi who said, 'On the day of judgment men will give an account for everything they should have enjoyed but didn't.' This book is a call to remember that 'everything created by God is good, and nothing is to be rejected if it is received with thanksgiving' (1 Timothy 4:4 ESV)."

Dr. Mark Scott

Director of Preaching Department and Professor
of Preaching and New Testament at Ozark Christian College

"Becoming a responsible, faith-seeking, value-driven 'adult' doesn't mean life should be boring and blasé! Jeremy Jernigan masterfully crafts a well-researched, engaging conversation about pursuing pleasure the way it was designed to be, delivering rich insight wrapped in humor. If you are not experiencing the joy you hoped for in any area of your life, *Redeeming Pleasure* is a must-read and will give you a much-needed paradigm shift to put down the guilt and grab hold of abundant life as it is meant to be lived."

Paul Angone

Author of *All Groan Up: Searching for Self, Faith, and a Freaking Job!*

"I affirm this book with an enthusiastic YES! Kudos to Jeremy Jernigan for having the motivation and insight to confront a fundamental misconception of how to live well, ultimately diminishing humankind. Jeremy's deep dive look into human behavior, God's intentions, and our fixation on pleasure is sure to cause many people to rethink how life is lived in our pursuit of 'the ultimate.' This intelligent yet accessible read cracks the code to human freedom and fulfillment by learning to avoid the pain induced by natural impulses and tapping the source of divine, extravagant pleasure."

Monty Kelso

Founder/Partner of The Slingshot Group

REDEEMING PLEASURE

HOW THE PURSUIT
OF PLEASURE
MIRRORS OUR HUNGER
FOR GOD

JEREMY JERNIGAN

WORTHY®
PUBLISHING

To my wife, Michelle,
my trusted friend
on this journey of pleasure.

CONTENTS

A TALE OF TWO MICE

LIKE MANY KIDS, I grew up with all sorts of animals as pets: dogs, hamsters, mice, rats, lizards, frogs, fish, snakes, turtles, and even an African land crab. But never cats. Each animal brought unique experiences and memories. I remember feeding the crab everything from goldfish to Cheetos. I remember catching a bunch of tadpoles and raising them in my backyard as my own, only to find one day they had literally grown legs and jumped away. And I remember the mice, rats, and hamsters all enjoying the running wheel.

I've always found it fascinating to watch those little rodents churning away on the wheel. They run. And run. And run.

I wonder, why do they run?

It looks exhausting to me, but I suspect they find some enjoyment in it. Otherwise, why would they do it? Maybe it's like a spin class for rodents. It allows them to get a good sweat on and work off the extra calories from all that food in their little dish. I'm sure there's a self-conscious rodent or two out there thinking, *Does this cage make my fur look fat?*

That's about the extent of my extrapolations concerning the running wheel, but other people take this thought further. Some folks have argued that mice run on the wheel because they feel stress and anxiety from life in a cage. From that point of view, all that running doesn't sound so pleasurable. Is the mouse wheel a form of pleasure or is it a sign of unhappiness?

There's a big difference between the two, but how do we know?

This isn't a question just for mice. It's the question we should ask ourselves today. Are the behaviors and choices we make signs of pleasure or signs of captivity? And what exactly are we captive to? Do the messages we receive daily bring us the pleasure we think they do, or do they merely reflect our captivity to something else?

Here I have to hand it to science. Never one to leave a question like this unanswered, two researchers from the Netherlands decided to find out. Creating an experiment any junior high boy would love, they set up running wheels in the outdoors to see whether wild mice would choose to run on them voluntarily. (It's fun to imagine two serious-looking people in lab coats walking through the forest with tiny running wheels.) Would the mice choose to run for pleasure or would they reject the wheels because they didn't need them to relieve stress?

The surprising conclusion they found was that "mice came to the wheels like human beings to a health club holding a spring membership sale."[1] Evidently, mice actually love running on wheels whether they are caged or living in the wild. It is indeed a sign of pleasure.

That answers our mouse question, but not our human question.

Is your lifestyle giving you the pleasure you crave? Or does it reveal your captivity to a way of life that doesn't deliver as you expected? You probably have your own knee-jerk answer to this question. But like the researchers from the Netherlands, we'll take some time to explore the issue to provide us with a more objective answer to our question.

But I do know this for sure: we don't need to settle for a counterfeit pleasure when the real version is available.

CHAPTER ONE

THE PURSUIT

PURSUING GOD THROUGH PLEASURE

"All get what they want; they do not always like it."

C. S. Lewis, *The Magician's Nephew*

PLEASURE.

We hear about it, we think about it, and we look for it. Constantly.

The search for pleasure consumes our world. In our experiences and interactions with others, we search out sources of pleasure. We judge an evening's success by how much we enjoyed it. We create and keep friendships depending on whether we get something from them. We pick our hobbies based on how much pleasure we get from them. Pleasure is a fundamental ingredient of how we live.

This pleasure-driven standard has given the idea of work a negative view since it often produces little immediate pleasure. Having a job forces us to practice delayed gratification because the money we make allows us to do the things we enjoy later. Were it not for the regular paycheck, most people would not continue to work for the satisfaction from the job itself.

Consider your own job. If you learned today you had won the lottery or you received a substantial inheritance and money would no longer be an issue for you, would you continue at your current job? Would you show up at work each day not because you need the money but because you enjoy it that much?

Pleasure shapes everything. As a case in point, there is a strong chance you are currently reading this on a digital device as opposed to boring old paper. In fact, half of American adults own an e-reader device.[1] These devices bring the pleasure of the moment to your fingertips (and sometimes make it tough to keep reading for any amount of time when you're holding a phone or tablet with so many other distracting apps).

The multitalented writer and philosopher Blaise Pascal captured this idea four hundred years ago when he used the idea of happiness to make the same point.

> All men [and women] seek happiness. This is without exception. Whatever different means they employ, they all tend to this end. The cause of some going to war, and of others avoiding it, is the same desire in both, attended with different views. The will never takes the least step but to this object. This is the motive of every action of every man, even of those who hang themselves.[2]

The last sentence especially makes the point. Pleasure drives actions, even to the point of a person committing suicide, which is seemingly far from pleasure. When the present moment lacks pleasure severely enough, ending all future similar moments would provide him what he seeks (at least in his mind). This is a sad example of how far we will go for our sense of pleasure.

The problem arises from the average person's inability to know where to look or how to find the pleasure he craves. Our culture presents a wide variety of options to choose from, so a person never has to fret about what to try next. Yet the results of feeling pleasure are never guaranteed. Chasing after pleasure quickly becomes a vicious cycle when the consequences begin to pile up or we realize what other pleasures we've negated as a result of our choices.

Shortly before his death, actor Philip Seymour Hoffman gave an interview in which he discussed pleasure. Specifically, he talked about his realization that his pursuit of pleasure never led to his happiness. Consider his conclusion: "I think I kill pleasure. I take too much of it and make it unpleasurable . . . There is no pleasure that I have not made myself sick on."[3]

That's a heartbreaking perspective from a man who experienced many of the world's most sought-after and hard to reach pleasures. Yet his pursuit of it made him sick. It would also lead to a drug overdose that ended his life. We feel the weight and sadness of his perspective, yet we also connect with his conclusion. We've had glimpses of it ourselves. Is this normal? Is this to be expected? Is this all there is?

Where is your pursuit taking you?

THE PREMISE

In our search to experience more pleasure, we have convinced ourselves of a powerful lie—that we can have ultimate pleasure whenever and however we want it. William Temple once said, "It is much worse to have a false idea of God than no idea at all." It is no surprise many people not only have a false idea of God but also a false idea of how to enjoy the way He created us and everything around us.

Here lies the problem.

Every pleasure, from simple to complex, exists within its own limits. To experience the maximum enjoyment out of any given pleasure, we must pursue it according to its design. Despite this truth, our culture sidetracks us into creating our own realities to suit our individual wants. That's the dominant instruction in our culture today. But in doing so, we cheapen the end result we want most.

Most non-Christians view Christianity as a religion consisting of a bunch of enjoyable actions to avoid doing. The opposite is true. God created boundaries around pleasure not to keep us from enjoying life but to show us how to get the fullest experience. God alone knows how to get the most from pleasure, and it involves certain guidelines to achieve this. As a result, it is important we understand why the pursuit of pleasure is a topic of concern for us all.

One of the reasons we get messed up in our understanding of pleasure comes from a belief that pleasure itself keeps us from a right relationship with God. That's partially true. But not for the reason we think. Consider your own views. Is God the dad who turns out the lights and shuts down the party just as it gets good? Or is God the dad who opens His house to host the party? Those are dramatically different views of God, and dramatically different views of pleasure. You're going to want to highlight or underline the next sentence (seriously, it pretty much sums up the book).

By pursuing pleasure on our terms, we actually experience less of it.

That's the deception of pleasure. Further, whenever we fail to live life as designed, and subsequently settle for less pleasure, we experience isolation from God.

This topic extends further than just the idea of pleasure itself. This is a discussion on one of the critical foundations of Christianity and whether a person can accept Jesus Christ. When we strive to experience a pleasure on our terms, we want control. We see a pleasure and we pursue it the way we want to. We don't care about anyone else's opinion or how our pursuit will affect anyone else. The opposite way to approach pleasure is to pursue it the way someone else recommends us to, which can often be at odds with how we would go about attaining it. This is what we each must wrestle with when it comes to whether we trust Jesus in the pursuit of our pleasures. To experience a pleasure in a way other than how you might normally want to shows submission to someone else's authority, in this case God's.

> By pursuing pleasure on our terms, we actually experience less of it. That's the deception of pleasure.

A person might want to move toward Christianity but not want to surrender control of how he enjoys what he enjoys. He thinks if he agrees to a biblical lifestyle, then he will miss the fullness of his experiences. In reality, the only way he can enjoy a pleasurable life is through realizing that God created everything and trusting that He knows how to enjoy His creation better than we do.

How a person experiences pleasure turns out to be a fundamental part of one's journey with God, or without Him.

When discussing pleasure, we must look at it from a balanced view, careful to explore its nuanced pros and cons. Our culture has turned *pleasure* into a highly charged word. For some, it's sexual, bringing with it ideas of wild debauchery and unspeakable fantasies. That's often combined with a healthy dose of shame and guilt. For others, it's something unattainable, no matter how badly you want it. These people conclude this life wasn't designed for us to enjoy it. For others, it's misleading and never materializes when you expect it. It's a game where the rules seem to change and, at best, we can only hope to be lucky to grab a few moments of pleasure here and there. The list could go on and on. Each person brings his or her own views into the discussion.

Pleasure itself is not bad. In fact, it's a part of creation that is unbelievably good. And it's a lot more than sexual, although I'll spend a chapter on that later (if you've already checked it out, that may tell you something about how you view pleasure).

Pleasure is a gift from God that He left subject to our individual choices. While I'm not sure how much we can control what gives us pleasure, we can certainly control how we pursue the pleasures we find. This is where culture corrupts our thinking. We make ourselves into mini-gods of our lives and allow ourselves the right to decide the terms of our pleasures. Despite this, we still find we cannot control as much as we'd like to think we can. The alternative—trying to eradicate our desire for pleasure—isn't a realistic option either. Author Peter Rollins wrote in *The Divine Magician*, "The desire to rid ourselves of desire is paradoxically a pursuit of death, for it is only in a deathlike state that desire and longing can be extinguished." As Rollins illustrates, the desire for pleasure is inherent to the experience of being human. We cannot and should not attempt to squelch it. We are then left to figure out what to do with this desire.

THE BIBLE SAYS

There's an old expression that goes like this: "God said it, I believe it, and that settles it."

It sounds cute and makes for a perfect bumper sticker (for those who think we should attempt to capture the Divine on the extremities of our vehicle). But for most people—myself included—this expression comes up dramatically short. I also think it makes people less inclined to hear what God actually said.

Is it wrong to ask why God said what He said *before* we believe it?

What if the answer to that question allowed us eventually to believe what we read from God in the Bible? What if a refusal to answer this question causes a person to dismiss God's instruction who might have otherwise believed?

This is precisely what is happening all around us. Christians are watching college students leave the church en masse. The president of the Barna Research group, David Kinnaman, addressed the discontent of the younger generation in his book *UnChristian* by surveying sixteen- to twenty-nine-year-olds.

That's where the term "unChristian" came from. Young people are very candid. In our interviews, we kept encountering young people—both those inside the church and outside of it—who said that something was broken in the present-day expression of Christianity.

In his book *The Great Evangelical Recession*, Pastor John S. Dickerson offered the following sobering facts:

- Multiple sources show that evangelical believers account for only 7 to 9 percent of the United States population.
- Of America's 316 million residents, we evangelicals only account for about 22 to 28 million . . . we lose about 2.6 million of those each decade.
- To put it in international terms, there are slightly more evangelicals in the entire United States than there are Muslims in the greater metro area of Cairo, Egypt.
- In separate studies Josh McDowell, LifeWay Research, the Barna Group, and secular researchers, including those at UCLA, have all landed at figures between 69 and 80 percent of evangelicals in their twenties who leave the faith.

Or consider the research quoted by James Emery White in his book *The Rise of the Nones*. The "nones" he refers to are Americans who claim no religious affiliation.

The number of nones in the 1930s and '40s hovered around 5 percent. By 1990 that number had only risen to 8 percent, a mere 3 percent rise in over half a century. Between 1990 and 2008—just eighteen years—the number of nones leaped from 8.1 percent to 15 percent. Then, in just four short years, it climbed to 20 percent, representing one of every five Americans.

A recent survey by the Pew Research Center showed more of the same. According to Greg Smith, the lead researcher on the project, "We've known that the religiously unaffiliated has been growing for decades. But the pace at which they've continued to grow is really astounding."[4] It's not hard to find evidence supporting this trend in America. Those statistics above are just a few.

Despite whether those of us who are Christians care to admit it, we have major problems on our hands. More of the same will produce less of what we care about. It's time for a new conversation.

We need to talk about why God directed us to live by a particular set of guidelines instead of allowing us to make our own rules indiscriminately. Teaching someone to trust God's unique way of living often falls on

> There are enough logical answers to the *why* questions that suggest God knows *what* He's talking about.

deaf ears. But I've found that when we begin by looking at *why*, we eventually get to *what*. I'm not saying we can apply logic to God and He suddenly makes perfect sense. I'm saying there are enough logical answers to the *why* questions that suggest God knows *what* He's talking about. A deep trust in Jesus is often the result, but trust makes a difficult starting point.

No doubt you've had at least one person in your life tell you something you *should* do. Maybe it was advice about whom to go out with (or when to break it off), which career path to choose, or how to navigate one of life's many forks in the road. The advice often comes from a trusted source such as a parent, spouse, or close friend. For many of us, at least one of those people followed their advice with the phrase "because the Bible says so." The cousin to this statement, often used with the first, is "because God says so."

Trump card one and trump card two.

This argument breaks down because of perspective, not because of its truth.

Let's suppose the Bible does say what your friend claims, or it is true God has said what they credit to Him. That's all fine and well. But what if you don't believe in God or trust the Bible as reliable? No matter how close you are to the person giving the advice, the two of you will quickly experience frustration and the tension that inevitably follows two contrasting worldviews. They decided their belief based on a foundational value you don't share.

It's like expecting every kid to act according to my family's rules. In my house, it's understandable to have this expectation. I don't let other kids stand on my couch no matter what they do in their own home. But when we are with friends at a restaurant, imagine if I were to reprimand someone else's child for failing to follow my family's rules. I'd get an odd look from my friend, and we'd have an awkward discussion about why I'm disciplining his child. They have a different family code.

We accept that the expectations of parenting are unique to each family. Whether it applies to bedtimes, food, daily routines, or boundaries, we understand this intuitively. This acceptance allows us to temper expectations of others and focus on what we alone control. With this understanding we can confidently interact with other parents.

It's simple with parenting but far more complex with decisions we make as adults. Consider our standard logic, which goes something like this: other kids need not act like my kids, but other adults should act like me.

In his book *The Righteous Mind*, Jonathan Haidt used the analogy of an elephant and a rider to describe what happens. The rider represents our reason, and the elephant represents our intuition. Here, reason stands for our carefully thought-out conclusions, while intuition is our immediate gut feeling. Haidt powerfully argued that while we'd like to think our intuitions follow our reasoning, the reverse is true. Our intuitions largely shape us and then our reason tries to make sense as to why.

If you don't believe in God, then your elephant will take you in the direction of discrediting what God or what the Bible says. If the person talking to you does believe in God, her elephant is taking her in the exact opposite direction. But we don't see that part. What we usually see, and focus the conversation on, is that your reason cannot make sense out of your friend's reason and the other way around. And these conversations rarely end well.

That's because one person's intuition (Haidt's elephant) starts them with the premise that God is real and worth trusting while the other person's intuition starts them with the premise that God isn't real or isn't worth trusting. The details of the discussion (Haidt's rider) are merely the symptom of a bigger cause.

Experience teaches us to avoid having a similar conversation with that person again. So when you have enough of these moments, you eventually stop having these conversations altogether. It should come as no surprise why we consider discussing politics and religion socially inappropriate.

This is perhaps the greatest reason we need a conversation like this. My hope is that by recognizing we are all riding on various intuition-elephants, we can best see the arguments in an objective way. Complete objectivity isn't possible, but I'm confident we can push past many conversations that have previously ended in frustration. At the very least, my hope is that we will see our own subjectivity more clearly.

If someone told me to do something because "the *Book of Mormon* says," they would likely feel disheartened by the perplexed look on my face in response. I don't believe the *Book of Mormon* contains ultimate truth, so why would I shape my actions according to it? Yet this is precisely how Christians tend to give advice to people when they fail to recognize the elephant that's currently leading them. It doesn't matter whether the book we argue for is the *Koran*, *The Bhagavad Gita*, *The God Delusion* by Richard Dawkins, or some other guide to your unique spirituality. When we fail to acknowledge another person's intuitions, we fail to win them with our reason.

My own elephant of intuition leads me to believe that both the Bible and the living God it shows us as Father, Son (Jesus), and Spirit are trustworthy. But I recognize my view may not be yours. You've already formed your opinions about the Bible and the God it portrays, and they may not be favorable. Please relax, knowing I'm not going to throw a bunch of "you should" and "you need to" spiritual arguments at you. You've heard enough of those, and we know those arguments have a horrible track record. Guilt only works for a season.

If your elephant is different from mine, I invite you simply to consider arguments from a different perspective. You don't have to share my beliefs to consider the following arguments. However, not only do I believe these ideas to be true, I also believe you can see them work in your life. This is an important aspect of this material, since as Andy Stanley argued, "People are far more interested in what works than what's true." I believe seeing past the deception of pleasure is both true and that it works, but I hope to show you first it works in order to eventually show it's true.

It's time to redeem pleasure.

For the college student debating whether to have sex with his girlfriend.

For the skeptic who feels a sense of God but can't make sense out of why.

For the Christian who wants to live life the way God intended her to live it.

For the person who believes in God but is afraid of what it would mean to follow Him.

For the person attracted to his or her same sex.

For the person overwhelmed by guilt and regret in his life.

I want to redeem pleasure for anyone pursuing pleasure and struggling to make sense out of God.

Whatever direction your intuition elephant is taking you, I hope this serves as a conversation starter for all of us. None of us want to believe something that isn't true, and that is a danger we share when our intuitions alone chart our primary course.

It may come as a surprise to learn the topic of pleasure has the ability to unite us. Regardless of your current intuitions, we share this same drive. As we see throughout history, it is a key part of what makes us human.

EPICURUS: OUR FELLOW JOURNEYMAN

An ancient Greek philosopher named Epicurus lived three hundred years before Jesus. Today Epicurus is often associated with hedonism, the school of thought that teaches pleasure is the greatest good. Epicurus taught his students about the pursuit of pleasure and how it affects all areas of life. While I do not align with Epicureanism, Epicurus serves as a great partner through our journey toward pleasure today. As a result, I will quote him as we go along to show how our discussion unpacks the same issues that men like Epicurus have wrestled with for more than two thousand years.

In a letter to Menoeceus, Epicurus argued the following:

> Therefore, we declare that pleasure is the beginning and the goal of a happy life. For we recognize pleasure as the first good and as inborn; it is from this that we begin every choice and every avoidance. It is to pleasure that we have recourse, using the feeling as our standard for judging every good.[5]

I think Epicurus nailed it here. Our pursuit of pleasure shapes life for us even if we don't think of it in those terms. In fact, few people do. While my conclusions differ from those of Epicurus, I admire him for his pursuit of understanding and I'm grateful for the perspective we gain from seeing his ideas on the same issues we wrestle with today.

There are also times when I personally connect with Epicurus's own journey. He once directed his followers to "send me a pot of cheese, so that I may be able to indulge myself whenever I wish." That's a man after my own heart!

Most readers will be unfamiliar with Epicurus, which allows us to start with a blank slate. However, to those who are already aware of him, you likely have a negative view of his life and teachings. It is helpful to consider the way the theologian N. T. Wright spoke of Epicurus as we begin our journey with him:

> Epicurus does not, however, deserve the sneers of those who considered him and his followers mere hedonists. It was a lofty, quiet sort of pleasure he had in mind, since bodily passions notoriously bring all kinds of bad long-term consequences. The ideal state of mind was ataraxia, "undisturbedness."[6]

Ataraxia is a Greek word that means "a state of freedom from emotional disturbance and anxiety."[7] It may be a good synonym for our search of pleasure from this point on. It's the notion of pleasure done right, without the consequences we tend to assume come with the territory. Instead of tasting just a fraction of the pleasure we seek, *ataraxia* is getting the full dose. It's true pleasure versus a fake, partial pleasure. It's following the shadow to discover that which cast it.

Before we are ready to see what this full picture of pleasure looks like, we must wrestle with its source. If God created pleasure, what we think of God will be connected to what we think of pleasure (I see my elephant just walked into the room). Our journey begins with Him.

WHOSE IDEA WAS THIS?

In his book *The Screwtape Letters*, C. S. Lewis provocatively created an opportunity for the reader to listen in on a conversation between a senior demon and a younger demon-in-training. In this context, the "Enemy" referred to is God Himself.

Never forget that when we are dealing with any pleasure in its healthy and normal and satisfying form, we are, in a sense on the Enemy's ground. I know we have won many a soul through pleasure. All the same, it is His invention, not ours. He made the pleasures: all our research so far has not enabled us to produce one. All we can do is encourage the humans to take the pleasure which our Enemy has produced, at times, or in ways, or in degrees, which He has forbidden. Hence we always try to work away from the natural condition of any pleasure to that in which it is least natural, least redolent of its Maker, and least pleasurable. An ever increasing craving for an ever diminishing pleasure is the formula.

Let's begin with the premise, as Lewis did, that God created pleasure and not Satan. Depending on your upbringing, this may be a challenging idea for you to accept. I know of many branches of Christianity that frown on behaviors like dancing, watching movies, and drinking alcohol. Some go further and even forbid them (there goes my Friday night . . .).

But we will begin our discussion by accepting that pleasure is not a threat to God. Pleasure does not disgust God. And God is not silent about pleasure. This is one area in which God has made His opinion known, which we will explore below. Sadly, most people today consider themselves informed while they hold on to misguided opinions of God. These views grow not from a desire to malign God, but rather they naturally permeate our thinking when we accept the dominant messages of the culture around us without question. If, as Lewis stated, the goal of this world is "an ever increasing craving for an ever diminishing pleasure," our goal is an ever increasing expectation for an ever increasing pleasure.

This topic goes as far back as the garden of Eden. It doesn't matter whether you think Adam and Eve existed as real people or they are symbolic of something else. What's interesting to me is that the first problem the Bible mentions humanity facing relates to pleasures. You may have heard the story as a kid, but in case you haven't, here is my two-sentence summary: God created utopia for a man and woman with unlimited pleasure at their disposal. All God asked in return was that they avoid eating the fruit of one tree.

Quiz time: Which tree was off limits? Some of you are thinking back to flannelgraph cartoon figures you saw as a kid. What did the fabric tree look like?

Your first guess might be a tree of evil, or a tree of pleasure, or a tree of life, or maybe it was just a stupid placebo tree God planted as a test.

The answer is that God forbade Adam (Eve wasn't around yet) to eat from the tree of the *knowledge* of good and evil.[8] Think about that for a moment. The tree wasn't evil; it simply gave them knowledge to judge good and evil.

> It doesn't matter whether you think Adam and Eve existed as real people or they are symbolic ...
> The first problem the Bible mentions humanity facing relates to pleasures.

Isn't that a good skill?

Isn't that what all good religious leaders and philosophers help us do? Doesn't that describe the entire self-help section at your local bookstore in a nutshell? Isn't that why you keep a mental checklist of the good behaviors and the bad behaviors you do each day in hopes there is more good than bad?

We learn from the opening chapters of the Bible that God never designed humanity to carry the responsibility of deciding good and evil. That's God's job. Whenever we put ourselves in that position, we sit in someone else's chair. As pastor and author Tim Keller succinctly put it in a social media post, "The fastest way to be like Satan is to try to be God. The fastest way to be like God is to refuse to be God in your life."

Deciding good and evil is beyond your skill set.

Some of you may have already highlighted that last sentence. Others may stagger at how politically incorrect it sounds. No, I'm not arguing that we check our brains at the door and robotically follow commands without thought. What I am arguing is that even in our most brilliant moment we cannot improve on reality. As the old expression goes, reality is what continues to exist after you stop believing in it.

You might push on this argument. It may appear that God simply gave them the knowledge of good and evil, not the ability to decide good and evil. But consider this, Adam knew that eating from that tree was wrong, or bad, or any other word you'd choose here to describe what God told him. He already had a basic knowledge of this. There was something else that the tree provided beyond just a literal understanding of information. It was rather that "eating from this tree would make Adam, not God, the determiner of right and wrong."[9]

It was a type of knowledge God didn't intend for Adam to have.

That's because he wasn't the Designer. Even if you believe the earth is the result of a random Big Bang followed by millions of years of evolution and that God played no part, you still know *you* are not the Designer. You don't have to believe in a designer to know you aren't it. C. S. Lewis wrote in *Mere Christianity*,

> God made us: invented us as a man invents an engine. A car is made to run on petrol, and it would not run properly on anything else. Now God designed the human machine to run on Himself. He Himself is the fuel our spirits were designed to burn, or the food our spirits were designed to feed on. There is no other. That is why it is just no good asking God to make us happy in our own way without bothering about religion. God cannot give us a happiness and peace [and pleasure] apart from Himself, because it is not there. There is no such thing.

The Designer's prerogative means that if there is a designer, He controls the rules of the game. He decides what is up and what is down. He decides the temperature that water freezes and the temperature that it boils. How arrogant!

But what if you wanted water to boil at 150 degrees Fahrenheit instead of 212 degrees because that would save you time staring at the stove? Too bad. You don't get to decide that. You aren't the Designer.

The Designer sets the boundaries and we decide how to respond. The Designer reveals the nature of good as He reveals Himself. When we follow the boundaries of the design, we experience the fullness that comes with it. We cook our meals according to the realities of nature and our Top Ramen tastes like a college student's dream. Conversely, when we try to place our own parameters into the design, we end up trying to make soup out of lukewarm water.

We don't get to answer the question of the temperature at which water *should* boil. Yet that is precisely what many people spend their life doing. They argue the merit of what *should* be and why.

Our question is much simpler: How would you like your soup?

AN INGLORIOUS GLUTTONY

Pleasure exists on many levels and in many varying degrees. Food is a basic pleasure we long to experience daily. As living beings, we want to pleasure our appetites and our taste buds while filling a reoccurring need in our stomachs. Let's begin with this most basic pleasure and expand it into more complex pleasures. As Epicurus said, "The beginning and root of all good is the pleasure of the stomach; even wisdom and refinements have reference to this."[10]

I'd guess Epicurus enjoyed food, and food is a good place to start our discussion. In John Calvin's *The Golden Booklet of the True Christian Life*, the famed spiritual leader argued that "if we study . . . why he has created the various kinds of food, we shall find that it was his intention not only to provide for our needs, but likewise for our pleasure and for our delight." In Calvin's view, God doesn't just meet needs but also brings us pleasure in the process.

Let's pretend there is a scale that can measure the ideal result in achieving enjoyment. From one to ten, a pleasure that we experience fully rates a ten for the person experiencing it. To get level ten from pleasure requires a person to follow the guidelines associated with that pleasure.

For example, a person wants to get a level-ten enjoyment out of a dinner she will make. For her to enjoy this meal, she must find a recipe that will create something that brings her pleasure, both to her appetite and her taste. She will need to find the right ingredients to fill the recipe's needs. She will need to prepare the ingredients and bring them together according to the manner in which the recipe describes. How effectively she does all this will determine how much she will enjoy her dinner.

Now, if the woman decides she wants her result (her pleasure) on her own terms, she can attempt to get it that way. She can make up her own recipe if she does not like her current one. She can leave out ingredients or substitute other ingredients. If she is on par with Mario Batali or some other Food Network star, she might possibly pull this off. I know my skills aren't there. I bake more like Mario and Luigi. So let's assume she's like me. If she is impatient, she can also skip the preparation time and eat the food before it's fully cooked or prepared. But in all of these cases, unless she's an excellent cook (and even that has its limits), she reduces her results. She cheapens her pleasure because she did not follow the guidelines. Some of you can think of a specific memory where this was your experience! It's like eating your favorite cereal with water instead of milk because it's "close enough."

If our person in the example above does not know how to create a recipe or decides to change the needed ingredients, then her chicken dinner could taste like rotten noodles or any other culinary nightmare. If she cannot wait to let her chicken cook properly, she might chew undercooked meat and find herself sick shortly after consumption. Her level-ten pleasure has now become drastically less enjoyable.

The deception of pleasure strikes again.

While we understand a one-time event like this (we've all been there), how foolish for our friend to continue eating every meal this way! At some point we'd want to shake her and try to get her to see this isn't the way food should be eaten.

Get out of the kitchen. Quickly!

Or consider Skyline Chili, one of my favorite meals. It's an Ohio-based chain of restaurants that I've sadly learned is an acquired taste. You can buy cans of Skyline Chili at the supermarkets where I live so I've had the chance to introduce this specialty food to many of my friends. The way I've learned to make Skyline Chili garners a bit of heckling whenever people watch it. If you've never had it before, consider the following recipe of mine a bonus to the book. For context, think of the Skyline Chili as more of a spaghetti sauce, rather than a traditional chili (it's thin and has a hint of cinnamon in it).

You start with a plate of noodles spread out, then add a layer of Skyline evenly across the noodles, finished with a thick layer of cheese on top. If you do it right, all you should see when you are done is a layer of cheese. If you see noodles or chili, add more cheese. You then eat it by cutting out bites and getting all three levels in one, not wrapping the noodles around your fork like traditional spaghetti. As you can imagine, this is far too strange and bizarre for the typical person to put up with and they either decide to eat something else, or butcher it with their own accommodations. I've tried this on enough people to have seen all matter of responses to it. But as I know with Skyline Chili, there is definitely a right way to enjoy it. Everything else lessens the experience.

Or think of one of your favorite restaurant. Likely you enjoy taking friends to it, especially for the first time. You probably have one or two things on the menu you recommend they order to get the full experience. You may feel a moment of pause if your friends decide to order something else on the menu that you've never tried. After all, you can't vouch for that item and it may jeopardize the opinion they'll form of the restaurant. I feel this tension every time my friend Roosevelt eats at Burrito Express with me and orders the nachos. Then again, maybe I just have control issues with food.

While it's easy to see the importance of design with food analogies, other pleasures in life are not as obvious. But before we can get to the design of pleasures, we must spend a few moments talking about our views of the Designer.

CHAPTER TWO

THE ANGRY GOD
IN THE SKY

PURSUING GOD
THROUGH CLARITY

"Beliefs matter. Bad beliefs hurt us all.
Good beliefs benefit us all."

Paul Stevens

BEFORE WE GET INTO THE DETAILS of the pleasures God created, we must spend a moment on our views of God, first looking at the negative ones we often associate with Him and then in the next chapter considering that He could actually be good. Each of these ideas set the stage for this argument on pleasure since the way we search for both pleasure and God is intertwined.

Many of us begin our conversations about God with a negative image of Him. Often people think of God as a crotchety old man with a beard, possibly holding a lightning bolt. This view carries more weight to us than we might acknowledge. I'm reminded of David Dark's powerful metaphor of Uncle Ben as God. He described a fictional group of people meeting together each week. Much of it sounds like a normal church gathering until a bell sounds and they all walk down into the basement to see Uncle Ben. It's worth repeating part of the interaction here.

They wait in silence. In time the man turns around. His face is angry, contorted. He fixes a threatening stare of barely contained rage on each person, then roars, "Am I good?"

To which they respond in unison, "Yes Uncle Ben, you are good."

"Am I worthy of praise?"

"You alone are worthy of our praise."

"Do you love me more than anything? More than anyone?"

"We love you and you alone, Uncle Ben."

"You better love me, or I'm going to put you . . . in here"—he opens the furnace door to reveal a gaping darkness—"forever."

Out of the darkness can be heard sounds of anguish and lament. Then he closes the furnace door and turns his back to them. They sit in silence.[1]

Although written with great imagery and detail from Dark, thankfully he doesn't believe this version of God to be accurate. Yet he acknowledged this view captures the prevailing sentiments some feel even if they can't articulate it this way. I find Dark's depiction of an "Uncle Ben god" both humorous and depressing.

I find the story humorous because it's so absurd. With his angry, contorted face, Uncle Ben threatens them after asking them the stunning question: "Am I good?" I almost want to laugh here, as the word *good* feels so wildly inconsistent with everything about Uncle Ben up to this point and everything afterward. There's nothing good we can find in Uncle Ben. He feels like an insecure tyrant struggling to maintain control. I'm reminded of the character Michael Scott as the regional manager of a paper company in the show *The Office*. As he reflects on his leadership style, he asks, "Do I want to be feared or loved? Um . . . easy, both. I want people to be afraid of how much they love me."[2] Uncle Ben captures that sentiment in a less funny way.

But I find the Uncle Ben depiction depressing when I realize it reflects how many people see God. It's telling that the interchange between Uncle Ben and the "congregation" starts and ends with them in a tense silence. There's nothing pleasurable about this experience. While Uncle Ben is not the God I see in the Bible, it's the God of the Bible to many people, especially in the United States. I'll readily acknowledge that if Uncle Ben was my view of God, I'd want nothing to do with Him. I shudder to think of how those with an Uncle Ben view of God see Christians.

I read the passage about Uncle Ben in a sermon recently. After the service, a mother came up to me and told me she came to church that day with her adult daughter. After I had read the quote about Uncle Ben, she leaned over to her daughter and told her that my illustration was absurd, since "nobody actually thinks of God like that." In an incredible moment of honesty, her daughter replied that Uncle Ben perfectly captured the way she viewed God.

This mom was stunned by what she learned from her daughter that day but was grateful for the chance to talk about it. If you also view God in an Uncle Ben way, I invite you to challenge that depiction as we go, and my hope is that your view of God will be transformed.

THE TEN COMMANDMENTS

Much of our thinking about a dry and demanding God stems from the Ten Commandments. This is God's supreme rule list for Him to grade us on.

I'm amazed how much divergent thought exists today about the Ten Commandments. Many Christians were ready to riot at the removal of the Ten Commandments from schools. These Christians think we must live strictly by each one of them today as the Israelites did when Moses marched down the mountain carrying them. Other Christians would consider them standards to live by. Still others say they don't apply to us today in the same way.

You may have seen a letter originally written to radio host Dr. Laura that has since become a viral sensation. It's commonly attributed to J. Kent Ashcraft, although it has appeared in different forms with different attribution. Specifically, he was responding to Dr. Laura's comments about criticizing homosexuality using the Old Testament. (We'll get to that in chapter 4.)

Regardless of its authenticity, I include a part of Ashcraft's letter here as it shows the contextual difficulty for Christians today in referencing the law of the Old Testament as a guideline for us to live by. It is long and worth searching for the whole letter online to read it in its entirety, but here are a few of the specific questions asked.[3]

I would like to sell my daughter into slavery, as sanctioned in Exodus 21:7. In this day and age, what do you think would be a fair price for her?

I know that I am allowed no contact with a woman while she is in her period of menstrual uncleanliness

(Leviticus 15:19–24). The problem is, how do I tell? I have tried asking, but most women take offense.

Leviticus 25:44 states that I may indeed possess slaves, both male and female, provided they are purchased from neighboring nations. A friend of mine claims that this applies to Mexicans, but not Canadians. Can you clarify? Why can't I own Canadians?

Most of my male friends get their hair trimmed, including the hair around their temples, even though this is expressly forbidden by Leviticus 19:27. How should they die?

Once we wade through the deep sarcasm, we can easily see the difficulty in many of the traditional arguments for God based on Old Testament scriptures and against relationships like gay unions. But this needn't present a problem for us. On this subject, my stand will likely make me popular with non-Christians and vilified by some Christians. Jesus had a tendency to do this so I'm comfortable following His lead.

I don't believe we live under the Ten Commandments today.

Before you throw this book into the trash (if you are reading this with an e-reader, please don't sacrifice it because of me), hear me out. That doesn't mean there is no value in them or that we can't choose to live by them voluntarily. But the law of the Ten Commandments does not apply to you unless you are Jewish or you choose to live under the entire law of the Old Testament rather than the new covenant of Jesus.

We can see why if we look at just a couple of biblical passages (not to mention Ashcraft's letter). The fourth commandment of the big ten is about Sabbath rest and has the longest explanation of all of them.

> Observe the Sabbath day by keeping it holy, as the LORD your God has commanded you. Six days you shall labor and do all your work, but the seventh day is a sabbath to the LORD your God. On it you shall not do any work, neither you, nor your son or daughter, nor your male or female servant, nor your ox, your donkey or any of your animals, nor any foreigner residing in your towns, so that your male and female servants may rest, as you do. Remember that you were slaves in Egypt and that the LORD your God brought you out of there with a mighty hand and an outstretched arm. Therefore the LORD your God has commanded you to observe the Sabbath day.[4]

Pretty descriptive, right? You have no idea. This commandment grew even more when the Israelites worked out the details of how to follow it. One time when I was in Israel I noticed they have a special type of elevator in addition to the regular ones. These are known as Shabbat elevators. When it's the Sabbath you don't have to push any buttons to get to your floor. It stops at each one of them. Modern-day Orthodox Jews consider pushing elevator buttons work. I think the real work is trying to find a regular elevator when you find yourself stuck inside one of these!

Sabbath means you do nothing even hinting at work from sundown to sundown for an entire twenty-four-hour period. Friday to Saturday. And you do this every week!

No e-mails.

No yard work.

No car maintenance.

No paying bills.

No catching up on your to-do list.

No laundry.

No lighting a candle or making a fire.

No doing anything resembling work.

Here's the point. Most Christians today who say we should live by the Ten Commandments don't come anywhere close to truly living by any of them if they are honest.

Give yourself the test by starting with the Sabbath commandment. Do you live with this level of Sabbath rest every single week of your life? Again, if we say we live under the Ten Commandments, we can't also say they are just the Ten Suggestions to follow.

It is law or it is not.

I preached about this once and explained I'd never met a Christian who followed the Sabbath the way the Old Testament law mandated. That week I received two e-mails from people letting me know they did indeed live like this and proved me wrong.

I e-mailed each back and asked if they had ever once missed the Sabbath. If they wanted to live under law, then they must live by what the law prescribes to do when someone breaks it. We don't have to wonder how to enforce a Sabbath breaker. God clearly stated that as well.

Observe the Sabbath, because it is holy to you. Anyone who desecrates it is to be put to death; those who do any work on that day must be cut off from their people. For six days work is to be done, but the seventh day is a day of sabbath rest, holy to the LORD. Whoever does any work on the Sabbath day is to be put to death.[5]

I asked them if they were going to follow that part of the law too. Since they obviously weren't, how did they justify following only part of it?

I never heard back.

You may doubt whether the Israelites ever actually killed someone over this. In another book of the Bible[6] we read about the Israelites stoning a man for collecting wood on the Sabbath! They meant business.

We don't stone people today, certainly not for doing a little work on the Sabbath. And we also don't follow the Sabbath the way God commanded it by law.

Is nine out of ten good enough?

If you are a Christian reader feeling disequilibrium right now, you are in good company. This is part of the journey of breaking free of cultural religion and experiencing God more fully.

The Ten Commandments are 10 of 613 instructions Judaism teaches. It's all or nothing if you want to give them the power of law in your life.

This doesn't mean it is suddenly okay to murder. We can look to the wisdom of those instructions without applying the obligation as long as we shift our thinking. All Christians do this today, even if they don't realize it. That's why we still wash our hands but don't lose any sleep over wearing clothes with mixed fabrics (both issues addressed by Old Testament laws).

The point is that the Ten Commandments are 10 of 613 instructions Judaism teaches. It's all or nothing if you want to give them the power of law in your life. Picking 10 (or 9) out of 613 is a faulty solution. Jesus summed up obedience to Him by teaching His followers to love God and love others. That's at least a bit easier to remember.

This is a powerful theological transition, yet is beyond the scope of what we need for our discussion. For more reading on this subject I'd recommend *The Naked Gospel* by Andrew Farley. Farley provides the most precise explanation of the simplicity of Christianity I have ever read.

One of the points of the Ten Commandments was to set apart God's people as special, for Israel to experience a better life than the nations around them. We see this context in the preceding chapter of Deuteronomy.

> Because he loved your ancestors and chose their descendants after them, he brought you out of Egypt by his Presence and his great strength, to drive out before you nations greater and stronger than you and to bring you into their land to give it to you for your inheritance, as it is today.[7]

God never intended the Ten Commandments to be a weight on His people. Rather, they were a way for them to experience a life with the pleasure of God's design and God's favor. God removed the speculation and showed them exactly how to live right with Him. When we live with them as a weight on us today, we apply something God never intended.

Later, Jesus would apply these commandments to show us our need for Him. We realize the amazing contrast of Jesus' offer of forgiveness once we've compared it to living under the law. The goal is to realize they are impossible to keep, not to try harder.

This is just a glimpse of why we call Jesus' message the Good News.

HELL: THE SPIRITUAL FOUR-LETTER WORD

Let's address the furnace part of the Uncle Ben narrative. After all, the concept of God's eternal punishment for His supposed enemies is a tough pill to swallow, yet it drives much of the motivation often given as to why we should follow God. Which for many people, myself included, is deeply problematic.

What do we do with hell?

Much ink has been spilled on this topic, and even Christians disagree with what the Bible presents as hell. In fact, taking any type of stance on hell quickly creates allies and enemies. Part of the challenge in discussing it biblically is there is much debate on the actual words used for hell in the Bible. Which words are literal and which are metaphorical? The idea of hell precedes even Christianity itself as the concept of hell (literally *Sheol*, or the grave) was part of the Jewish faith.[8] In the New Testament (written originally in Greek) we see three different words that most English translations render as hell.[9]

For those of you with little experience with the Bible, please humor me for a moment. I'll try to show some of the complexity that makes it difficult for us today. We often hear hell enter the mainstream with books like Rob Bell's *Love Wins*. The controversy and success of that book lost him support of many Christians (Bell used to be pastor of a church in Michigan), yet also set him up for his current speaking tour with Oprah Winfrey. Then of course there are the views to rebut Bell's. Then there are those Christians of the Calvinist persuasion who see hell as a sign of God's sovereignty, as He is the only one who can decide who goes there (regardless of our free will). These are just a few of the examples where we see the diversity of thought on this subject. And that's just the Christians.

The traditional view of hell is known as *eternal conscious torment*, or ECT for short. This view holds that while the saved people party in heaven for eternity, the unsaved lost souls suffer an ongoing torment. This view is often problematic for both Christians and non-Christians alike. How is heaven enjoyable if we know people we love are suffering? How can God enjoy eternity with us when He knows that people He created and loves are suffering forever? Or consider a Jew killed in the Holocaust who rejected Jesus Christ as his savior. Does he escape the horrors of the Holocaust after he dies only to enter far worse horrors for eternity?

We might wonder whether a few hundred years of this type of hell would allow a person to "pay their dues" for whatever they did on earth, even people like Hitler. Wouldn't even the most angry and vengeful among us admit there is a point when enough is enough? We might consider that in our American courtrooms today the two harshest penalties are execution or life in prison (which is not necessarily enjoyable but far from an ongoing physical torture). As extremes, neither of these earthly punishments even come close to the traditional view of hell. The traditional ECT view of hell combines an eternal life-sentence while also adding to that a perpetual torture at the same time. If any major government proposed a life sentence with perpetual torture for a prisoner today, we'd see instant outrage and protest over it from the rest of the world.

Not surprisingly, this view dramatically shapes our view of God. Uncle Ben emerges as the result.

While we don't need to definitively work through the details of each view, let me offer one view that you might not be familiar with. My hope is that this gives you a way of thinking of the biblical concept of hell without it mandating an Uncle Ben concept of God. Personally, I tend to side with the annihilationism view of hell (this view is also called conditionalism).[10] Don't be scared off by the long words. This is the perspective that in His mercy, God ends the soul's existence in eternity for those who reject Him. I find this view the most consistent way to look at eternity in light of the entire narrative of Scripture. In this view, just as we ceased to exist before we were born, those in hell cease to exist after their life on earth.

But what about those verses that mention "eternal" punishment? In this light, while the results of annihilationism are eternal (they forever cease to exist from that point on), the punishment and suffering aren't eternal (there is no red devil stabbing them continually with a pitchfork, or nothing with the creativity of Dante's *Inferno*). In fact, in the Bible we sometimes see the afterlife referenced as people falling asleep after death. Thankfully, the ECT view of hell isn't our only biblical option. Here are a few examples where we see the annihilationism argument made in the Bible:

1. "Behold, all souls are [God's]; the soul of the father as well as the soul of the son is [God's]. The soul who sins will die" (Ezekiel 18:4 NASB).

2. "Just as you drank on my holy hill, so all the nations will drink continually; they will drink and drink and be as if they had never been" (Obadiah 1:16).

3. "How suddenly are they destroyed, completely swept away by terrors! They are like a dream when one awakes" (Psalm 73:19–20a).

4. "His winnowing fork is in his hand, and he will clear his threshing floor, gathering his wheat into the barn and burning up the chaff with unquenchable fire" (Matthew 3:12; also Luke 3:17).

5. "Do not be afraid of those who kill the body but cannot kill the soul. Rather, be afraid of the One who can destroy both soul and body in hell" (Matthew 10:28).

6. "After [Jesus] had said this, he went on to tell them, 'Our friend Lazarus has fallen asleep; but I am going there to wake him up'" (John 11:11).

7. "After that, [Jesus] appeared to more than five hundred of the brothers and sisters at the same time, most of whom are still living, though some have fallen asleep" (1 Corinthians 15:6).

8. "But Christ has indeed been raised from the dead, the firstfruits of those who have fallen asleep" (1 Corinthians 15:20).

9. "So will it be with the resurrection of the dead. The

body that is sown is perishable, it is raised imperishable"
(1 Corinthians 15:42).

10. "I declare to you, brothers and sisters, that flesh and
blood cannot inherit the kingdom of God, nor does
the perishable inherit the imperishable. Listen, I tell
you a mystery: We will not all sleep, but we will all
be changed—in a flash, in the twinkling of an eye, at
the last trumpet. For the trumpet will sound, the dead
will be raised imperishable, and we will be changed"
(1 Corinthians 15:50–52).

11. "According to the Lord's word, we tell you that we
who are still alive, who are left until the coming of the
Lord, will certainly not precede those who have fallen
asleep" (1 Thessalonians 4:15).

While not the majority Christian view on hell today, we see
this view argued by the early Christian apologist Arnobius of Sicca
as far back as three hundred years after Jesus. It would be hard to
describe the typical Uncle Ben–type furnace-hell as a place where
someone falls asleep or where their soul simply dies. As a result,
consider how much the annihilationism view of hell alters our
view of a vengeful God. We needn't view hell as God's attack dog,
baring its teeth and growling at us, leashed up until a future date.
Hell is the logical result of our choices. John Stackhouse Jr. offered
perspective on this view of hell when he reflected,

Wouldn't it be reassuring not to have to try to bend one's
mind and, worse, one's heart into a shape that could

somehow give glory to God for afflicting people forever, that could somehow call majestic what seems obviously monstrous?[11]

As I've mentioned above, this is certainly not the only Christian view of hell, and there are other passages in the Bible that offer other possibilities. Regardless of the details, there are two important conclusions to keep in mind.

First, God doesn't send people to hell; we choose it. This may sound crazy, but if heaven is the fullness of the presence of God, it would literally be hell for God to make a person go there who has intentionally spent his or her life avoiding Him. Just as God does not force Himself on a person in this life, so also God does not force Himself on a person for eternity. Eternity is God honoring our decisions on earth forever. As Tim Keller put it in *The Reason for God*, "Hell is simply one's freely chosen identity apart from God on a trajectory into infinity." Hell has nothing to do with making the Father God mad and being eternally grounded for it. Hell is the choice we make (and God honors) when we decide we want nothing to do with Him.

The second important conclusion on hell is that the Bible clearly states there is no salvation apart from Jesus Christ. While the specifics aren't as clear, this part definitely is. Salvation through Jesus even applies to people in the Old Testament who lived before Jesus of Nazareth came on the scene.[12] I submit this shows us that salvation through Jesus applies even to some people today who might not have heard the literal name of Jesus. However Jesus does the saving, it will be Him doing it.

- "Jesus is 'the stone you builders rejected, which has become the cornerstone.' Salvation is found in no one else, for there is no other name under heaven given to mankind by which we must be saved" (Acts 4:11–12).
- "Jesus answered, 'I am the way and the truth and the life. No one comes to the Father except through me'" (John 14:6).

This is why Christians passionately share their views of Jesus with others. We want people to experience the same goodness of Jesus Christ we have. Eternal life, both now and forever, is only found in relationship with Him. The alternative is non-life, as it were, which some experience now on earth and some experience in eternity.

If hell sounds unappealing to you for eternity, it should sound unappealing to your life now. If you wouldn't want eternity without God, why would you want to live without Him now? Conversely, if hell sounds appealing to you for eternity, it should sound appealing to your life now. If you want your life without God now, you should also want your eternity without Him.

> If you wouldn't want eternity without God, why would you want to live without Him now?

If that logic doesn't ring true in your life, I'd encourage you to take a moment of reflection. I've found that many people think they want eternity with God yet they don't need to live with Him now. This makes no sense. Consider your own views. Does your desire for eternity match your desire for life now? While I'd caution us from getting lost in the details, the premise is of the utmost importance. Ideas have consequences. Ideas shape actions.

If you do want to experience eternal life instead of hell, there's good and bad news. The bad news is you'll never be good enough to make that happen. Seriously, stop trying. The good news is you don't have to be good enough. That's why Jesus died to provide a way for us to experience eternal life with God. I love the unique way author Donald Miller described this in *Father Fiction*: "Heaven and hell are about who you know, not what you do." But here again, we must provide some perspective on that process in order to avoid a view of Uncle Ben.

How do we *know* this Jesus in a way that brings salvation?

CHRISTUS VICTOR

A key concept in the Bible is something Christians refer to as the atonement. It speaks to the idea of God reconciling humanity back to Himself after we had gone our own ways, and I think most of us can acknowledge we have. Therefore, we experience a separation from God. We each have to respond to this dilemma if we decide we want to try to get back to God (even no action is a response). The Bible shows us that God has already chosen His response to remedy the separation.

Even if you have little to no experience with theology (the study of God), you've likely considered the question: Why did Jesus have to die?

Unfortunately, many think God the Father is an angry, wrath-filled judge who demands payment. He's angry at us for our sin. Here Uncle Ben comes to mind. But then His own Son, Jesus, came and paid the tab we ran up, thus satiating God's need for blood. There are many problems with this view, even biblically.

The apostle Paul said that "God was reconciling the world to himself in Christ."[13] It wasn't God the Father versus God the Son. They were seamlessly in harmony with one another.

And logically, it doesn't take much to realize this completely defies the concept of a good God. It's difficult to argue that a really good God also happens to have a bloodthirsty rage and so He made His own Son die as a result.

If you've been a Christian for many years, it may be difficult for you to see how others could have this point of view. Think of it in practical terms. If you knew a dad who forced his child to die because he was angry with the world, would you argue he was a good dad? Especially if that dad was somehow happy, or at the very least wasn't all that angry after his son died?

Yet this is how many people make sense out of what happened with Jesus on the cross. In fact, this is often *the* issue why many people decide they can't follow God.

But it doesn't need to be.

> In a nutshell, our sin sells us into spiritual slavery to the powers of evil, but Jesus buys us back on the cross.

A lesser known view of the atonement is something called *Christus Victor*. It's a Latin phrase that means "Christ is victorious." In this explanation, the focus is Christ's victory over the power of Satan, not God's appeasement. Our mistakes and failures, what the Bible refers to as sin, put us into slavery of the devil. Critics might argue this view turns us into mere victims, but this need not be the case. When it comes to our separation from God, we are the guilty ones, but our guilt has consequences that extend far beyond us.

In a nutshell, our sin sells us into spiritual slavery to the powers of evil, but Jesus buys us back on the cross. Just a few verses before the passage we looked at from the apostle Paul, he explained it this way: "And having disarmed the powers and authorities, [Jesus] made a public spectacle of them, triumphing over them by the cross."[14] The author of the book of Hebrews said it like this: "Since the children have flesh and blood, [Jesus] too shared in their humanity so that by his death he might break the power of him who holds the power of death—that is, the devil."[15]

The biblical authors show us it was Jesus versus Satan, not Jesus versus the Father. This distinction alters our view of God dramatically. The author and theologian Greg Boyd said it this way:

> In the Christus Victor view, Jesus died as our substitute and bore our sin and guilt by voluntarily experiencing the full force of the rebel kingdom we have all allowed to reign on the earth. To save us, he experienced the full consequences of sin that we otherwise would have experienced. In so doing, he broke open the gates of hell, destroyed the power of sin, erased the law that stood against us, and thereby freed us to receive the Holy Spirit and walk in right relatedness with God.[16]

One of the best analogies of atonement I've ever seen comes from the 2008 movie *Gran Torino* with Clint Eastwood. It may seem an unlikely example for me to use as it includes a significant amount of language and racial slurs. If you can look beyond this (and it's difficult at times), you'll see the story of a bitter Korean

War veteran named Walt. He's experienced his fair share of loss (the movie opens with the death of his wife) and he clings to his prejudices for his identity. The storyline focuses on the fact that the neighborhood is quickly changing around him and he's now forced to deal with his prejudices in tangible new ways.

Walt owns a 1972 Gran Torino car in mint condition. It's one of the few things in his life that brings him any pleasure. When a neighborhood boy named Thao (a young Hmong teenager) tries to steal it, Walt eventually finds himself in the position to help the teenager on the right path. This causes Walt not only to relate with but to defend this unlikely friend. In particular, Thao needs defending from a local gang. Walt learns that Thao's attempt at stealing his car was Thao's botched initiation assignment for the gang.

At one point in the movie, Walt makes the observation that Thao and his sister, Sue, are never going to find peace in this world as long as the gang is around.

Suddenly, the hardened old man begins to care for this kid on a whole new level. He's not content until Thao experiences genuine peace. So he thinks of ways in which he can provide a solution. We get a moment of foreshadowing in a conversation Walt has with the local priest, who asks him what he's going to do. "Whatever it is, they won't have a chance," says Walt.

In most Hollywood movies, many of those with Clint Eastwood, we'd likely expect Walt to dust off his .44 Magnum handgun and take care of the gang *Dirty Harry* style. It would involve slow-motion animations, lots of explosions, and a liberal amount of blood. But not in this movie.

In one of the most powerful climactic scenes in cinema, Walt steps out on behalf of Thao in vulnerability. He confronts the gang at their house—unarmed—and is killed in the process. But this stunning act of courage draws out and exposes the gang for what they are. It is this shocking reversal that brings freedom for Thao and punishment for the gang. Walt achieves victory through surrender instead of might.

That's what Jesus did on the cross, not just for a couple of teenagers, but for all of mankind. In partnership with the Father and the Spirit, He willingly chose to expose the devil's plans. In the process He rendered Satan's power over us obsolete and empty. Christ is victor above all through the stunning act of sacrifice and surrender. But unlike Walt, His life was far from over. It was Friday, but Sunday was coming.

About seven hundred years before Jesus, the prophet Hosea foretold it like this:

> I will deliver this people from the power of the grave;
>   I will redeem them from death.
> Where, O death, are your plagues?
>   Where, O grave, is your destruction?[17]

The victor mocks death itself. Not because He overpowered it in a grand show of might, but because He surrendered to it, exposed it, and lived to ensure it would have no more power in our lives unless we chose it. I'm sure it stunned Satan in the process.

That's how a good God fights. Satan never had a chance.

At Walt's funeral, the priest reflects on his life:

Walt Kowalski once said to me that I knew nothing about life or death, because I was an over-educated, 27-year-old virgin who held the hand of superstitious old women and promised them eternity. Walt definitely had no problem calling it like he saw it. But he was right. I knew really nothing about life or death, until I got to know Walt . . . and boy, did I learn.

Oh, and amidst the shock and confusion of Walt's remaining family, he ends up leaving his Gran Torino to Thao in his will.

THE MORAL POLICE

Should we follow God only from fear of the consequences of not doing so? Or should we only follow God if we want the rewards? If we hinge our actions solely on the consequences or rewards as it applies to our view of God, we are being reactive instead of proactive. The goal should be to follow pleasure at its core. It's that simple.

We should not be living to avoid an angry version of God. I've met many Catholics who have spent years doing just that. Eventually, the guilt and shame become unbearable. That's because whether God exists or not, there is still a best way to live a life of true pleasure. This will look different for each person to some extent. One person may find pleasure in the color blue and another person finds pleasure in the color red. But if blue is your thing, choosing red will cause less pleasure for you. Pleasure itself is a consequence of our choices. For that, we must consider the design of our pleasures, regardless of whom or what designed them. It doesn't even matter if you credit it to Mother Nature or the evolutionary process. The more we follow the design of pleasures the more we experience them in their fullness. Your eyes see color in a certain way. It isn't all relative. You need to learn that way and why in order to enjoy blue to the fullest.

Consequences and rewards should be seen as by-products rather than the aim of pleasure.

Let's pause a moment and consider a question for any Christian reading this. Would you live differently if you believed God doesn't exist? I asked the following question to the readers (mostly Christian) of my blog: "If I could prove to you (and you believed me with certainty) that God didn't exist, would it change the way you live? If so, how?"[18]

Some of their answers are telling:[19]

If you could prove to me that God didn't exist at this point in my life, it would devastate me! But would I no longer care about what anyone thinks or the consequences of my actions, returning to [my previous life]? NO! Because in all my years here on this earth, I have seen and suffered the fallout from people living a self-centered life, devoid of any accountability or standards. Their selfish actions spread like a cancer, infecting all in their path. That's not a life for me, with OR without God. *(Deborah)*

Since the way I was living before my faith grew was only seeking my own happiness, I would have to say that God is the only reason I willingly don't seek my own way. If I knew there was no God, I would have no reason to give up having my own way. I know I would be more prideful and self-centered. I'd be living it up as often as possible or I'd be depressed because of my circumstances. *(Kaylene)*

Over time, I would most likely fall away from being Christlike, start drinking again, maybe enjoying a few nights out on the town, slowly slipping back to my old life. It would be a slow fade nonetheless, one that would ease off the teachings of this so called Jesus. I could only imagine it as growing down instead of up. So, because of that vision of how my life might turn out if "I thought" God didn't exist, I would have never wanted to know in the first place. Don't kill my buzz man! Please warn me if you ever prove He doesn't because I DONT WANT TO KNOW! *(Steve)*

The answer would be different at different points in my life. Fifteen years ago, I would lose hope and simply choose the worldly way, because there would be no plan B. I'd be on a selfish path, still looking for the bigger better party, trying to achieve worldly success. In REALITY, that indulgence would bring discontent, trying to fill a hole only God can fill, BUT if God did not exist, would it bring contentment? At this point in my life, would I really change course that much, knowing that His way is the best way, and by taking the *His* out of His way, would I just continue *that* way? I could go on and on about the implications. Life would have no meaning, no purpose, no value. All those things exist because God exists. Again, it's truly an impossible question. *(Lisa)*

I do not think it would change anything. Based on your premise, there would be no need for a relationship with Him, so prayer and Bible study would leave my normal routines. But I would still maintain the principles taught by the Bible because they still work. I have an amazing marriage because I put my wife's needs before my own and my children are growing up in that environment, which teaches them to do the same. To change that would be to my detriment. We follow biblical financial principles that keep us from wrecking our financial future. Were your premise true it would still not change the truth of biblical philosophy. And comparing my life to my acquaintances who believe as you suggest, I can tell you I am far more content, healthy, and happy than they. *(Alex)*

My point in asking this question is not to create an impossible alternate reality (if there's no God, then there's no Bible, then there's no . . . etc.). I think this question gets to the heart of why people follow God in the first place. It's fascinating to me that even Christians don't agree on the answer. And that's just five of the responses I received.

I have pondered my own answer and think that if I came to the realization that God doesn't exist, and I knew it with certainty, I'm sure I'd still live the way I currently do. To quote Lisa, I'd still live "that way."

I would still be faithful to my wife. I would still lead with integrity and strive to be a trustworthy person. I would still do my best every day to put the needs of others before my own, especially with my family. I would still look for ways to be generous to others and challenge myself to sacrifice for others. As Alex said, "I would still maintain the principles taught by the Bible because they still work."

All of these actions bring me a deep sense of pleasure in my life. It happens as a natural result. Said differently, they are the consequences of my choices. This is not to negate the point the apostle Paul made when he said, "If Christ has not been raised, our preaching is useless and so is your faith."[20] My faith would be null and void, as would the hopes I hold. My outlook on life would certainly change. But the natural consequences of my lifestyle would remain the same.

My point here is you don't have to start with a belief in God. That's where the discussion ends for many people. Rather, when you start by looking at the design itself, it eventually leads you to God.

Similar to the person looking at the endless stars in the night sky and deciding there must be a God, when we look at the design of our pleasures, we look to a great Designer. When all we focus on is the Designer, we end up having a harder time understanding the design of our pleasures. That's why so many people need to reframe this conversation.

Maybe God isn't as bad as you thought He was. But could He actually be good?

CHAPTER THREE

COULD GOD
REALLY BE GOOD?

PURSUING GOD
THROUGH HOPE

"If you were to always act in your greatest
self-interest, you would always obey God."

Mark Batterson

IF WE ACCEPT THAT GOD is the Designer of pleasure (there's that
elephant again), it stands to reason that our view of God dramatically shapes our pleasure. After all, if we don't get past the angry
god in the sky we saw in the last chapter (Uncle Ben), we'll have a
difficult time associating anything that comes from Him as pleasurable. That's why a book on pleasure must also have a focus on
the nature of God.

In God's design of the world, He created pleasure. We might
think this means He is above it or beyond enjoying His creation.
But here's a twist: God pursues pleasure too.

Not only are God and pleasure not mutually exclusive, God
also aims toward the same goal! God travels the same journey we
do, but He travels it differently. Namely, God enjoys Himself.

This is possible because He is complete in Himself. Many
people borrow a famous line from the movie *Jerry Maguire* when

it comes to love: "You complete me." That sounds romantic, but it isn't true. Ask any married person and you'll quickly see people can't complete people. You can destroy many a relationship trying to prove this. Only God can complete people. God completes us because He doesn't need anyone or anything to complete Him.

We see an incredible picture of this in the opening words of the Bible. After laying the foundation for creation, God gets ready to make humans. The Bible communicates it this way: "Then God said, 'Let us make human beings in our image, to be like us.'"[1]

Who is this "us" and "our"?

Christianity explains this as the Trinity, one God in three parts: Spirit, Son, and Father. But don't let that confuse you. The point is the Bible depicts a God who can enjoy Himself. A God who needs nothing and who pursues nothing to fill His own emptiness. He exists in community with Himself. He experiences love because He isn't alone.

Because of this, He can invite us into His completeness. We aren't a means to an end. This is where our pleasure comes from. The best way for us to experience pleasure is to join in God's pursuit of it.

CHRISTIAN HEDONISM

Each of us has people in our lives whom we grant special access to speak into the foundations of what we believe. For me, these usually consist of writers and preachers. My connection comes both from their style and their content. I try to allow my group of personal influencers to be as diverse as possible.

I say all this to set up an idea from John Piper, a preacher and writer whom I don't normally align with. Coincidentally, I once quoted him on my blog and it snowed where I live in Arizona that same day. When social media exploded with comments on the crazy weather (snow in the desert?) and people asked what on earth was happening, a friend of mine chimed in that it was because I had quoted John Piper!

Hell was literally freezing over.

Piper's particular theology and style deviate from my own in most areas. But he coined a brilliant term in his book *Desiring God.* According to Piper, Christian hedonism refers to the idea that "God is most glorified in us when we are most satisfied in Him." He continued his explanation by stating, "I came to see that it is unbiblical and arrogant to try to worship God for any other reason than the pleasure to be had in him."

What a crazy, good idea!

The seeds of this phrase precede Piper. St. Augustine used this same premise in his famous definition of love: "By love I mean the impulse of one's mind to enjoy God on His own account and to enjoy oneself and one's neighbor on account of God."[2] This shows us that for many years, Christian thought has incorporated a proper view of pleasure as it relates to our spirituality.

By contrast, standard hedonism is the pursuit of pleasure above all else. Or that all pursuits in life are ultimately about pleasure. What people like Augustine and Piper argued is a natural connection of two ideas that go together despite sounding contradictory. A Christian hedonist does not chase pleasure at the expense of God, but chases pleasure through the pursuit of God. This happens only when we break through the deception of pleasure we have created. God and pleasure are not mutually exclusive. Rather, God holds the keys to pleasure.

Likely, your experience with God, or how you've seen others experience Him, has little to do with pleasure. It usually involves rote obedience, dry discipline, and guilt-driven morality. But this was never God's intent. When we experience God without pleasure, it's like holding a snakeskin and convincing yourself you are holding the snake itself.

Imagine someone holding a snakeskin and then warning you to be cautious of the snake's potential to bite you. While the skin shows the overall shape and size of the snake (at least the moment it shed that skin), it transmits none of the life or power the snake holds. The same is true of God.

A pursuit of God without the pleasure of God is legalism. As Major Ian Thomas once said, "I know of nothing quite so boring as Christianity without Christ." I'm not interested either. Yet this accurately describes the way many people follow God. Is it any surprise then that many people use the word *boring* to describe religion?

> When we experience God without pleasure, it's like holding a snakeskin and convincing yourself you are holding the snake itself.

I've often talked with non-Christians who describe their view of God to me and then I tell them that I wouldn't follow Him either if I believed what they believed. Our view of God, like our view of pleasure, matters immensely. Finding pleasure in God creates the environment to follow Him well. It's like a surfer putting wax on the bottom of her board. While it doesn't suddenly change the nature of surfing, it makes it easier for the surfer to do what she attempts to do with the board.

This doesn't mean obedience is always sexy. My selfishness

continues to make it a daily struggle to serve those around me, even when it's my family. But experiencing God through pleasure is the difference between happiness and joy. If all you pursue is happiness, you will likely avoid unhappy moments that would eventually lead you to joy. But if you pursue joy, you can endure unhappy experiences for the greater outcome you'll experience. I experience the pleasure of the relationships with my family because of my willingness to sacrifice for them moment by moment.

God and pleasure are not mutually exclusive, but a short-sighted perspective causes us to overvalue a moment and undervalue a lifetime.

Surprisingly, in our search for this basic need, we have the greatest potential for spiritual unity. You may not consider yourself much of a spiritual person. But as the musician Michael Gungor once said, "Religious belief is kind of like sexual orientation—everyone has it. Even not having a preference is a preference in itself."

Your path to pleasure shapes your spirituality. And it shapes the way you interact with the people around you and your view of God.

A KINGDOM OF NOW AND NOT YET

Here are two different ideas, which seem mutually exclusive but are both true: (1) this world is a broken place; yet (2) God is good. We might assume *if* God is truly good, *then* the world shouldn't be a broken place. Or we might conclude *if* the world turns out to be a broken place, *then* God cannot be good. However, the health of our spirituality results from our ability to see past both of them.

My wife, Michelle, and I became foster parents just over a year ago. The foster journey has been a chance for us to plunge ourselves into an area of brokenness. And we have experienced a level of brokenness beyond what I had imagined. Our lives now intersect with people I'd normally not find myself around all that often, and this has provided a great perspective for my spirituality. I'm given a daily reminder of the broken world in my interactions with the many people involved with our foster child. They suffer through challenges most of which I've never had to deal with. I'm reminded of hardship through their point of view.

But this can quickly become overwhelming.

Just this week I felt the need to encourage my wife after I sensed the heaviness of the hurt in this world taking a toll on her. It fills her mind and overwhelms her emotions. This is why many people who sacrificially give of themselves for others often burn out in the process. I reminded her that this is but half of the equation.

The other reality is that the God we see in the Bible is a good God. That's not to say He doesn't do things beyond our explanation or understanding. Yet for Christians, our conclusion is that God is indeed good. And this is a truth we need to celebrate and respond to accordingly.

But this can quickly become isolating.

We can develop a taste only for goodness and therefore find ourselves filtering out anything else. The American Dream lulls many Christians into closing their eyes to the hurts around them. We put Jeremiah 29:11 on enough bumper stickers until we convince ourselves that God cares primarily about our prosperity. We isolate ourselves through Christian music, Christian books, and Christian friends. And then we become people others cannot seem to relate to anymore. If your toughest prayer request involves your difficult Pinterest projects, you might need to adjust your lens to the world.

Some people want to focus only on the brokenness in the world and allow themselves to fault God, Christianity, and any form of the church in the process. Doing this can cause you to feel overwhelmed with life. Other people want to focus only on the goodness of God and close their eyes to the many manifestations of brokenness they see around them. This will cause you to feel isolated.

We can err in either direction. The first step comes from realizing where you naturally lean and finding people and opportunities that help you live more balanced between the two. A good God has allowed us enough free will to sufficiently break much of the goodness in creation, yet He positions His people to display a kingdom of not yet into now. There's a part of eternal life that happens now, but there is a bigger redemption coming. God invites us to translate heaven to earth and bring hope into the despair of now.

THE MAGICIAN'S NEPHEW

One of my favorite fictional series is the Chronicles of Narnia from C. S. Lewis. It is a set of seven books detailing the land of Narnia and the humans who visit it. The rich symbolism of the story connects us uniquely to our own journey with God. The stories begin (chronological, not publication order) with a book called *The Magician's Nephew*.

That story details how the talking lion named Aslan, the character who represents Jesus, speaks (or rather sings) Narnia into existence. We experience the many facets of emotion through the eyes of different characters. We see purity and innocence through the eyes of little children watching and the adult cynicism and complexity through a character named Uncle Andrew.

When Uncle Andrew realizes this new land is fresh with life and possibilities, he immediately thinks of ways he can exploit this for his gains. Uncle Andrew, lost in his own world of greed and self-centeredness, cannot see the beauty of what is happening around him. When one of the children grows concerned about Uncle Andrew's motives, Aslan's response speaks volumes into our journey with God.

> "He thinks great folly, child," said Aslan. "This world is bursting with life for these few days because the song with which I called it into life still hangs in the air and rumbles in the ground. It will not be so for long. But I cannot tell that to this old sinner, and I cannot comfort him either; he has made himself unable to hear my voice. If I spoke to him, he would hear only growlings and roarings. Oh Adam's sons, how cleverly you defend yourselves against all that might do you good!"

That last line should cause us pause. How carefully do we defend ourselves from God? And how carefully do we defend ourselves from good? When we pursue pleasure with blinders to the beauty of the design around us, we limit ourselves to a small and lonely existence.

We each play the part of Uncle Andrew.

Yet here is God, singing a beautiful song of pleasure around us, if only we can hear it. How sad when all we hear is growling.

THE GOOD SHEPHERD

As a kid growing up in the church, I've heard the image of God as a shepherd for as long as I can remember. It's always been a safe idea that brings us comfort. Search Google images for the word *Jesus* and you'll see Him holding a baby sheep as one of the top results. It makes us think of Jesus as harmless.

The original idea of Jesus as our Shepherd comes from Jesus Himself. He once referred to Himself as not only a shepherd but a "good shepherd."[3] If you grew up in church like I did, you've likely never given this much thought. If you're hearing this analogy for the first time, it might not mean much to you since you likely don't interact with too many shepherds. But it's valuable to explore what point Jesus was making when He used this image.

To answer that question, we need to look to the original Jewish audience who heard Jesus call Himself this. What came to mind for them when He referred to Himself as a shepherd? The answer to that question is fascinating.

The Jewish concept of shepherds starts all the way at the beginning of the Bible. The first two people the Bible records—Adam and Eve—had two boys named Cain and Abel. In a subtle detail that's easy to overlook, we learn that "Abel kept flocks, and Cain worked the soil."[4] That means Abel was a shepherd and his brother, Cain, was a farmer. They both brought sacrifices to worship God, but God liked Abel's better because he gave his best. In true brotherly fashion, this made Cain furious with jealousy. He decided the best

> When we pursue pleasure with blinders to the beauty of the design around us, we limit ourselves to a small and lonely existence.

remedy for his anger was to kill his brother. The first recorded murder in biblical history is a farmer killing a shepherd.

The conflict between shepherds and farmers continues today. After all, they both have mutually exclusive uses for land. A farmer will cultivate it and plant on it for years. A shepherd will use it and move on to greener pastures. You cannot have them share a space effectively.

We see this escalate again when a guy named Joseph found himself down on his luck. His brothers sold him into slavery, and after a few roller-coaster years, he became the right-hand man to Pharaoh in Egypt. A severe drought brought many people to Egypt, including the very brothers who had betrayed Joseph. To make a long story short, he ended up forgiving them and inviting them to move to Egypt. But there was one problem. The Egyptians were a farming culture, and Joseph's brothers were shepherds. This had Cain and Abel written all over it. So what did Joseph do? He shrewdly coached his brothers on what to say and do so they were allowed to live in Egypt.

> Then Joseph said to his brothers and to his father's household, "I will go up and speak to Pharaoh and will say to him, 'My brothers and my father's household, who were living in the land of Canaan, have come to me. *The men are shepherds*; they tend livestock, and they have brought along their flocks and herds and everything they own.' When Pharaoh calls you in and asks, 'What is your occupation?' you should answer, 'Your servants have tended livestock from our boyhood on, just as our fathers did.' Then you

will be allowed to settle in the region of Goshen, *for all shepherds are detestable to the Egyptians.*"[5]

As a result, Joseph's brothers and their families, who became the beginning of the nation of Israel, received a land of their own in Egypt. Joseph's wisdom prevented the tension between farmers and shepherds from becoming an issue.

Many years passed, and eventually a pharaoh came to power who knew nothing of Joseph and what he had done for Egypt. Pharaoh realized the Israelites, who were still primarily shepherds, had become so numerous that they were a threat to him culturally and politically. So he made them slaves to the Egyptian farmers, and again we see the farmers with the upper hand. However, God called a man named Moses to lead these Israelites into a land of their own.

After a dramatic series of events (including ten plagues), the Israelites left Egypt and wandered through the wilderness for a generation. Eventually they received a land of their own, and then the biblical role of shepherds began to decline. The Israelites became farmers themselves.

As the years passed, the role of shepherds continued to diminish. There was one significant exception to this: a man named David who became only the third king of Israel.[6] In speaking to David, God said, "I took you from the pasture, from tending the flock, and appointed you ruler over my people Israel."[7] Essentially, God plucked David from obscurity and made him king. But David never lost his roots as a shepherd, which caused him to relate with God as a shepherd.

David was the one who wrote Psalm 23 about God being our shepherd. This has become one of the most quoted passages of Scripture today. While the psalm brings comfort, we miss the complexities of it when we assume David's view was reflective of how the Israelites viewed shepherds. David's view was unique. As the scholar Dr. Joachim Jeremias noted, "The rabbis ask with amazement how, in view of the despicable nature of shepherds, one can explain why God was called 'my shepherd' in Psalm 23:1." The prevailing sense of shepherding at that time was a negative one.

- In other passages God talked of destruction in terms of ruining property so it will only be useful to shepherds.[8]
- The prophet Amos told his own life story from rags to riches about how God pulled him from being a lowly shepherd and elevated him to the role of a prophet.[9]
- God used the image of a shepherd to help the people understand how He felt about the selfish religious leaders who were leading them.[10]

A lot of shepherds earned this poor reputation, while others fell victim to a harsh stereotype. To be fair, it was a difficult job. It required being gone for months at time. It involved danger from wild animals and robbers. As a result, many who had large flocks hired people to act as shepherds for them. These hired hands were likely the worst ones. Many of them intentionally led the flocks into areas owned by farmers and then abandoned them. The struggle with farmers continued.

Eventually, Israel made rules that further alienated shepherds. The rabbis banned pasturing sheep and goats in Israel, essentially creating a cultural smoking section farther away from the masses. They even made it illegal to buy certain items from shepherds on the assumption they would be stolen property. Shepherds couldn't fulfill a judicial office or appear as a witness in court because nobody would believe what they said. In the *Mishnah* (Judaism's written record of the oral law), shepherds are referred to as incompetent, and it was even stated that if a shepherd fell into a pit, no one was obligated to rescue them. Imagine that! You could pass by someone in distress without feeling any guilt if that person was a shepherd. They literally became a subclass of people.

Why, in view of all this, would Jesus ever attach the image of a shepherd to Himself?

Jesus used the flawed image of a shepherd to contrast the limitless nature of His own goodness. He's so good He's even a good shepherd (which many might have thought to be an oxymoron). That's why David's psalm about God as a shepherd says, "[His] *goodness* and *love* will follow me all the days of my life."[11]

Jesus is good.

He's better than you can imagine.

He's even better than you could hope for.

He's so good He can redeem the idea of a shepherd with all of the thousands of years of baggage it brings.

GOD WANTS TO PLEASURE YOU

Does the above heading creep you out?

I bet it does, because it felt weird for me to write it. I even had some friends encourage me to omit the heading from the book. Regardless, I believe that to be a true statement so I'm leaving it in. *Take that, all my friends who read early versions of my manuscript!*

Our negative reaction to this heading shows us the degree to which we've sidetracked our understanding of what pleasure means. And yes, I include myself.

When it comes to life-fulfilling pleasures, only God can satisfy. We may be able to get partial pleasure out of our small desires, but when we look at living a fulfilled life, only God can please us. We can see God's intent in the book of Isaiah: "The LORD will guide you always; he will satisfy your needs in a sun-scorched land."[12] God wants to satisfy us. In his book *Pursued*, Jud Wilhite stated that "God's presence is endless pleasure."

This chapter speaks into the pivotal issue that determines whether this is a book you read and move on from, or whether this is a book that will be a line in the sand for you. If God is good, and if God wants to bring pleasure to your life, the best thing you can do is follow His methods.

Recently my wife and I took our oldest son to a baseball game. I'm a bit of a baseball fan. Actually, I'm a huge baseball fan. Each of our kids has a middle name from a Yankee player. I'll give you a moment to wrap your mind around that.

> We may be able to get partial pleasure out of our small desires, but when we look at living a fulfilled life, only God can please us.

Our oldest son is Gavin Mattingly Jernigan. The name comes from my favorite Yankee player when I was a kid, Don Mattingly, who was the first baseman and captain for the Yankees and then coached with them for a bit after he finished playing. Currently he is the manager of the Los Angeles Dodgers.

The Dodgers play the Cubs in spring training in Arizona each year, and my wife and I thought it would be great for Gavin to meet the guy he's named after. We had been trying to connect Gavin with Don for multiple years. Last year when we went to a game, it turned out to be a split squad that day and Don was with the other half of the team.

This year we tried again. And this year Gavin met his name.

We got to the park nearly an hour early, before any other fans filled our section, and sat in the Arizona summer. Waiting. And waiting.

As a four-year-old, Gavin didn't fully understand what we were doing. He lasted about five minutes and then started hounding me to take him to do something else. I explained to him repeatedly that we had to wait by the dugout and be ready for the moment.

Dad had a plan.

But despite all of Gavin's effort, he just couldn't wrap his mind around it. So he asked me to walk around. He asked me to get him peanuts. He even asked me if it was time to go home.

What I knew, and Gavin didn't, was that if we had done any of those things, we could have missed our chance to have an incredible moment together. A moment I will remember as long as I live.

I just needed Gavin to trust me.

Before the first pitch was thrown, Don Mattingly emerged from the secret tunnels and out into the dugout. I was ready for him and leaned over the railing so he could see me. Trying not to sound like a total stalker, I shouted out that my son's middle name was Mattingly and asked if he would get a picture with us. Yelling to a stranger that you named your firstborn child after him is a strange experience. He looked up at me with a laughing smirk and agreed without hesitation.

Don walked over to us and shook hands with Gavin. In that moment I realized I'd just become dad of the year. My son was stellar. Like a champ he told him, "Nice to meet you." I think Don was a bit taken back by how well Gavin speaks for a little kid. Not only did Don pose for a photo, but he then asked me if I had a ball for him to sign.

That's when I realized I had made a colossal mistake. We had a great plan. But no baseball! I began imagining how Gavin would explain this experience to his counselor in later years.

I reluctantly told Don I didn't have a ball. Without skipping a beat, he called into the dugout for one of his guys to bring him one. I was stunned. This guy is the real deal.

Then Don, with a faint smile in the corner of his mouth, asked me if I had a pen to sign the ball with. That was just mean.

He then borrowed a pen from someone in the crowd and wrote this message on the baseball: "Gavin Mattingly, all my best, Don Mattingly." I was back to dad of the year again, thanks to Don.

I'm still trying to explain to Gavin why we can't play catch with his new ball.

Gavin is young enough that even though at times it's a struggle, he intuitively believes I have his best interest at heart. One day when he's older I'm sure he'll challenge this. But for now, he tries his best to be patient and trust his dad. He knows I want to bring him pleasure and satisfaction.

God wants the same for you. But sometimes it means you have to wait with him in the summer heat. As Jud Wilhite stated in *Pursued*, "Only when we make God the object of our worship will we then find all the things that we were searching for in our pursuit of money, love, sex, family, career, and status."

Our Dad has a plan.

Consider the following words from Jesus: "The thief comes only to steal and kill and destroy; I have come that they may have life, and have it to the full."[13] Jesus presented an idea that would surprise most people. God wants us to have life to the full? We see this idea all throughout the Bible. When we get past the false ideas of God from Hollywood and the poor examples of some Christians, we begin to see a story God has been telling throughout history.

It is a story that tells us God is for us, not against us.

It is a story about how God personally cares about every single one of us.

When we get down to it, our problem isn't that we want pleasure too much but that we don't want it badly enough. We settle for far less than the full life God intended for us.

Consider Epicurus. This man-of-pleasure had a surprisingly low standard: "The voice of the flesh cries, 'Keep me from hunger, thirst, and cold!' The man who has these sureties and who expects he always will would rival even Zeus for happiness." Epicurus considered a lack of hunger, thirst, and cold to be the fullness of life.

Jesus told a better story.

Epicurus also said, "I revel with pleasure in the body, living as I do on bread and water; I spit on extravagant pleasures, not for themselves but for the difficulties that attend them."[14] Like Adam and Eve found out in the garden, trying to gain extravagant pleasure by our own designs comes with difficulties. Sadly, many people accept those difficulties.

But that isn't life to the full.

Life to the full is the realization that on the outside you may not be any better off than the next guy. You may never keep up with the Joneses. But life to the full means it doesn't matter. You live each day with satisfaction, with hope, and with purpose. The pleasure of each day is more akin to joy than happiness.

But how many of us ever live this life? Life to the full looks drastically different from what many people expect in life.

CHAPTER FOUR

MATTRESS MAMBO

PURSUING GOD
THROUGH SEX

"Every man who knocks on the door
of a brothel is looking for God."

G. K. Chesterton

You KNEW A BOOK WITH THE WORD *pleasure* on the cover had to have a chapter about sex. Maybe you even jumped to this chapter without reading the rest of the book.

I get it.

I'll earn the "progressive" label for many of the ideas in this book, but my conservative stance on sex might seem surprising. Where I see unnatural limitations applied to so much of Christianity today, when it comes to sex, the parameters make sense. As Pastor Scott Sauls argued,

In fact, as Scripture unfolds from Old Testament to New, while it becomes more progressive in the way it dignifies, empowers, and liberates women, ethnic minorities, the enslaved and the oppressed, Scripture takes on a more conservative tone in the way it speaks of sex and marriage.[1]

As we do with each pleasure, we must independently examine sex in light of God's design. Sex is an often misused pleasure or, at a minimum, an area we rarely think critically about. My friend Trevor says there are many Christians who live as "sexual atheists." By that he means they trust God in every area of their lives except their sexuality. That's a sad and illogical way to live.

God created sex with specific guidelines. The author of Hebrews said, "Marriage should be honored by all, and the marriage bed kept pure."[2] The Greek word for *bed* in that verse is *koite* and often serves as a metaphor for sex in marriage. It's not just the bed itself but what happens on the bed. We're not talking about the difference between the bed at a five-star hotel and the bed of that hotel room you got the incredible deal on. That victory is short lived once you climb inside the covers. Instead, this becomes a symbol of something sacred. Today, the idea of a "marriage bed" seems like something you'd see at a museum or on a tour of an ancient culture. But biblically we see God established the intent of sex for a married relationship.

Unfortunately, our society paints the image of a biblical marriage in a dull light. Following scripture means saving yourself sexually for only one person and waiting to have sex with that one person until committed before God in marriage. People see these guidelines as archaic and limiting. I'm surprised how many times I've heard someone use the analogy of trying on a new shoe or test-driving a car for sleeping with someone before they get married. They argue abstinence may be one of the stupidest decisions a couple could make.

But consider that to make this point we compare people to shoes and cars, both utility items we use and then get rid of after they wear out. When I'm on my deathbed, I'm confident I'll have thrown out any shoes or gotten rid of cars I had on my wedding day, but I will bet anything my wife will be by my side.

In the world's eyes, sex only for marriage drastically reduces the pleasure because people cannot enjoy it as much as they want, whenever they want, and with whomever they want. How could this biblical view compete with the worldly pleasure of sex? By far, most of our entertainment presents sex in a nonbiblical way. Thus, the Christian ideal seems obsolete and outdated since those who follow the world's view get everything Christians have and more.

And that is where the deception works so brilliantly. The Bible refers to Satan as the father of lies for good reason.[3] The truth presents a different story than what the world would have us believe.

Consider what a person chasing sex in a worldly way has to deal with that a married woman having sex God's way never would. A woman having sex out of wedlock has to worry about getting pregnant when she cannot support a child or does not wish to take on this responsibility. She has to think about sexually transmitted diseases and constantly worry whether she has contracted something that will stay with her for the rest of her life or something that will end it far too soon. She will constantly try to prove herself and validate her worth to each new man she is with while competing against previous experiences she's had as well as her partners have had. And probably most overlooked is the enjoyment of this pleasure. She will look for a sexual experience with person after person, hoping it will keep getting better.

It can be a lifetime of one-night stands.

Epicurus's opinion on this specific topic is surprising. He argued that "sexual pleasure has never done anybody any good.

One must be content if it has not done actual harm." For a man who hunted pleasure professionally, this is not the stance we'd likely expect. Maybe Epicurus was bitter over a heartbreak or the one who got away. Or maybe, even in his lifetime's pursuit of pleasure, he realized sex outside of marriage has the potential to severely mess you up. Epicurus's school, known as The Garden, allowed both male and female students and practiced a lifestyle away from the public eye. As a result, some of his critics accused his school of secretly hosting orgies. Who knows how much or even what type of experience Epicurus had with sex. Whatever it was, it left him unsatisfied.

I don't know about you, but deciding I should avoid sex at all costs is a very unpleasurable stance to take! I'm grateful we don't have to agree with Epicurus's experience on this one.

Consider this: a married couple who enters their union as virgins will never have to compare their experience to former partners. They will never have to worry about whether they were as good as previous experiences. They only know each other! That is an expectation I'm comfortable with meeting.

> Deciding I should avoid sex at all costs is a very unpleasurable stance to take! I'm grateful we don't have to agree with Epicurus's experience on this one.

You may have heard a single man talk about how incredible it would be to sleep with a porn star. Seriously? Imagine trying to impress someone with that type of experience without any emotional connection or commitment as a foundation. Good luck. Whether he could admit it to himself or to others, he would question his own abilities and value.

Or, as anyone who has ever had sex knows, there is an unbelievable vulnerability that one enters with the sexual experience. Physical nakedness is just one aspect. Sex outside marriage brings an awkward tension of being this vulnerable with strangers or people who don't have a lifetime commitment to you. How many of our movies, TV shows, and cultural jokes refer to the "morning after"? When this is the norm, the best way to cope with it is to make light of it.

Vulnerability is a liability for sex outside marriage but a blessing to sex within marriage. A married couple builds on this vulnerability and finds themselves growing closer together in unspeakable ways over the years. The awkward tension of vulnerability leads to intimacy and acceptance.

Intimate sex beats casual sex.

In the book of Genesis, we read about how God created the world as we know it. Don't get lost on the details. The intriguing part is the verbiage used and how it connects to the topic of marriage.

In Genesis, the emphasis is on separation. God separates day from night, waters above from waters below, dry land from sea, and heavens from the earth. Everything has its boundaries, and the boundaries are what make it unique. Separation is the key.

We intuitively feel this to be true. In fact, for many people, separation is the defining characteristic of their life.

Many years later, Jesus did something remarkable to connect back to this concept. In the gospel of Matthew we read about a conversation where Jesus referenced creation and then made this statement about marriage: "So they are no longer two, but one flesh. Therefore what God has joined together, let no one separate."[4]

Jesus gave us a unique perspective that marriage is unique in joining two people together. This is an incredible truth if we are willing to consider it.

Studies have tried to capture the unique blessing this joining creates. In July of 2012, the *New York Times* released a powerful article titled "Two Classes, Divided by 'I Do.'"[5] The article showed through research and case studies the difference marriage has on kids. According to the article, almost half of unmarried parents living together during a child's birth will split up within five years. The article's author, Jason DeParle, cited numerous experts with extensive study on the effects of marriage. Consider the following two quotes:

- "It is the privileged Americans who are marrying, and marrying helps them stay privileged." —Andrew Cherlin, Johns Hopkins University sociologist
- "The people who need to stick together for economic reasons don't. And the people who least need to stick together do." —Christopher Jencks, Harvard sociologist

Even when we struggle to put our finger on why, we must admit the benefits from two people joined together. We can point to practical benefits such as dual incomes, dual perspectives, and shared responsibility. In today's world, though, you don't need to be married to experience these benefits. But there is still something more. Even though we like to separate the spiritual from the practical, they weave in and out in inseparable connectivity. Marriage brings tangible and intangible benefits. These benefits begin with the practical and spiritual joining together through sex reserved for this relationship.

Sociologists, such as the two I quoted above, like to focus on what they can tangibly measure. Christians like to focus on what they see happen but can't explain. Somehow we know they are both right.

What God has joined together.

I'll never forget a conversation with a close friend of mine whom I'll call David. David was a former musician with a child out of wedlock, but he now enjoyed his marriage and career in a large corporation. David had a past filled with sexual exploration that rivaled anything you've seen or heard from Hollywood. His band had enough success to tour regularly. David told me how he would sleep with a different woman every night of the tour as they went from place to place. But he had left that all behind for his marriage to an attractive wife and a more normal lifestyle.

One day, when I asked David how things were between him and his wife, he stunned me with his answer. He told me that his wife wanted to have sex all the time. I considered for a moment how many men would love to be able to say this about the woman they are with. But David had no desire to have sex with her. This confused me, and I asked him why. I'll never forget his answer.

"Because there is no challenge in it."

For my friend David, sex had become a way for him to prove his value and an adventure to test his abilities. He had lived it up in all the glory sex could bring. Sure, none of those one-night stands fulfilled him, but he knew there was always another one the next day. Now, as a married man, the conquest was over. All he had to do was find enjoyment in his readily available wife.

But he couldn't.

To David's credit, he didn't talk about his past as if it were the glory days. He was the first to admit how empty and shallow those sexual experiences were to him. He wanted something more. But his past had so distorted him he couldn't enjoy what was right in front of him. I'm reminded of what Rob Bell said in his book *Sex God*:

> Sex is not the search for something that's missing. It's the expression of something that's been found. It's designed to be the overflow, the culmination of something that a man and a woman have found in each other. It's a celebration of this living, breathing thing that's happening between the two of them.

It should come as no surprise that David and his wife are no longer together. He continues his search for pleasure elsewhere. That's because he's searching for something that's missing instead of celebrating what he had found. How many people today live with this same reality?

It seems God knew what He was doing when He set the boundaries. The married person's enjoyment of sex as God created it far surpasses any other way a person would try to fill this need. In the well-known 1994 Chicago study on human sexuality, they found results that are tough for most people to explain:

> We are left with a picture that does not fit any of the popular images . . . Those having the most partnered sex and enjoying it the most are married people . . . In real life,

the unheralded, seldom discussed world of married sex is actually the one that satisfies people the most.[6]

Science shows us that chemicals aid in this explanation. During sex, we release a chemical called oxytocin that allows us to bond with the other person. This is part of God's design for two people to join as one. It isn't a coincidence that substance is also found in a mother's breast milk.

According to researchers at the University of California, San Francisco, oxytocin is "associated with the ability to maintain healthy interpersonal relationships and healthy psychological boundaries with other people."[7] The more sex a couple has, and the more oxytocin released, the stronger the bond. Further, it aids in preserving a couple's committed relationship. According to a study cited by the *Journal of Neuroscience*:

In [a] randomized placebo-controlled trial, we provide the first behavioral evidence that the intranasal administration of [Oxytocin] stimulates men in a monogamous relationship, but not single ones, to keep a much greater distance . . . between themselves and an attractive woman during a first encounter.[8]

In addition, there's another chemical called vasopressin that helps guys in particular with the bonding process. This is more than just what we feel on an emotional level. Our bodies kick into a bigger design. But what happens when two people have sex without the commitment? What if all you have is casual sex with new people? Your body starts to adjust and causes the chemicals to stop working as originally designed. After enough of this experience, you lose the ability to bond to the other person through sex like you should.

Our attempts to change the design only hurt us.

THE BUBBLY BANKER

You ever have those days when you feel sucked into your to-do list? When the thought of enjoying the day drops far below a determination just to feel productive? Thankfully, most of my days aren't like this. But like you, I have moments like this.

When I published my first book, *Crowdsourcing the Message*, my accountant recommended I open a new checking account for the proceeds. A visit inside a bank ranks somewhere slightly above a trip to the DMV for me. Nonetheless, I walked into the bank one day and a bubbly teller in her twenties greeted me by the door. When I told her I was there to open a new account, her face lit up and she offered me a bottle of water to begin our conversation. Obviously we approached this interaction from dramatically different perspectives. And my routine errand began transforming into more.

She led me to her workstation. Her desk was part of a row of cubicles containing little walls to separate each station. We began the transaction, and I gave her my forms of identification while she started typing frantically at her computer. Without looking away from her screen, she asked me why I was opening a new account.

"I'm about to release my first book," I said. She flashed the same contagious smile I had already seen when I told her why I was originally there.

"What's your book about?" she asked. I stumbled with how to

explain collaborative preaching. "I wrote about the model we use at our church for writing the weekend messages." Simple enough explanation, I thought.

"That's cool," she calmly said and went back to typing. Without redirecting her gaze from her screen, she added, "So are you a full-time writer?"

"No, no," I said. "I work at a church." A sense of pride filled me that she assumed I could make a living from writing. At least I looked the part.

"Wait, you're a *pastor*?" I italicize the word *pastor* as it is the only way I know to explain how it sounded dramatically different from the rest of her sentence. The word lingered on her lips a moment too long, hesitant to join the conversation. She said it like she was discussing an endangered animal she had read about but never seen.

Now abandoning her computer, she leaned over her desk to ask me all manner of questions about our church and my role there. I gladly answered each of them and gave her the behind-the-scenes perspective on how it works. To my surprise, she looked fascinated by this.

She told me how she and her boyfriend had recently discussed how they wanted to stop going to the Catholic church and start going to a different kind of church, one like mine. While that may sound like an encouraging comment for her to make, her words struck me as the token response people give when they find out they are talking to a man of the cloth.

Eventually our church discussion ended and I gave her the final details she needed from me for my new account. Then she directed me to walk over to the counter behind me to make my deposit and bring her back the receipt. After a few moments I returned to her desk, expecting to close our time together. That's when she ramped things up a notch.

"Can I ask you a question?" She was leaning in again, and her eagerness made me cautious about what was coming next. I slowly nodded consent.

"What do you think about premarital sex?"

Here is a young woman, surrounded by her coworkers (remember the little walls), asking an incredibly sensitive question to a total stranger. The shock from her question sent me reeling to regain my composure.

Consider her question yourself. How would you respond to her? I'll tell you how I did in a minute.

This story illustrates for us the problem many people live with daily. She might decide she enjoys pleasure, and her natural impulse is to fulfill that desire. But she also realizes some pleasure proves less favorable when consequences occur. Until she learns to navigate these complexities, she will walk her road to pleasure without a guide and stumble frequently along the way.

Most people live like this every day.

We drink till we don't remember it or until we do something out of character. We view sex as a common way to connect with new people we meet and as a necessary part of dating. We experiment with substances for escape or just for fun. We eat to fill an appetite beyond our hunger for food. We sit and stare at our TV for hours each day to relax. We check our social media feed or our favorite entertainment magazine to dwell on other people's lives. We spend countless extra hours at our job each week in order to prove ourselves. We exercise obsessively in hopes of achieving the body we crave. We go out each night trying to fit in with friends or find "the one." We fall into debt buying stuff to establish our status with those around us. We spend hours in front of the mirror getting our look just right. We cross the line in relationships with people other than our spouse. The list goes on and on.

We fulfill our desires in numerous ways every day, often wondering if there's a better way. What exactly are we looking for anyway? What's really at the end of that fabled yellow brick road?

My bank teller was discussing her sex life with a complete stranger (not to mention a bank customer). Her question revealed she likely doubted her way of experiencing it outside of marriage. You may have doubted your own ways of pursuing pleasure as well. What do we do with that nagging feeling we are missing out or that there's something more?

Back to her question.

There are at least four insights I already knew about her that raced through my mind. First, she looked to be in her late twenties. Second, she had a boyfriend. Third, she grew up Catholic. Fourth, she was interested in what a pastor thought about sex outside of marriage. It didn't take Sherlock Holmes and his powers of deduction to infer she probably lived (and slept) with her boyfriend and felt a degree of guilt about it.

If you are a Christian, your advice would likely consist of quoting a verse to her or referencing what God and the Bible say about premarital sex. That's an understandable response. Her dismissal of that answer would be understandable as well.

If you are not a Christian, you might offer any number of

responses. One extreme would be to tell her she should live it up and never look back. Go to Jersey Shore and don't stop till you look exhausted, tan, and your clothes are all clean. But she wouldn't have asked you because you aren't a pastor (sorry for dropping a trick question on you).

So what did I say?

Instead of quoting the Bible or giving her a "you should," I laughed and told her I applauded her boldness. I then told her how I imagined she felt about it. She probably had plenty of guilt and was second-guessing her lifestyle yet was unsure what needed to change. In response to my observation, she nodded her head in quick agreement like Dr. Phil had just gazed into her soul.

> God designed sex with boundaries for us to experience it fully. Like all pleasure, sexual enjoyment hinges on its purpose and design.

My answer to her was simple: if she was having sex outside of marriage, she wasn't enjoying sex to the fullest. I asked her what she thought about the purpose of sex, but she didn't have an answer (I'm going to go out on a limb and assume she wasn't trying to start a family). I replied that God designed sex with boundaries for us to experience it fully. Like all pleasure, sexual enjoyment hinges on its purpose and design.

To the degree we experience pleasure by its design we experience the most from it. It's an understated idea that our life experiences prove to us time and again. And yes, the Bible does speak about it.

But don't just take my word on it.

SEX LIKE FIRE

A simple analogy here is useful. Like many other men I know, I learned I was a pyromaniac early in my childhood. Something about fire just relaxes me and soothes my soul. It's incredible how you can sit around with friends and stare into a fire together. Words aren't needed. The flames of a healthy fire bring something mystical to any gathering.

I've enjoyed many a good fire in many different ways. I think of the backyard fire pit that I've had many friends over to my house to enjoy with me on a winter evening. I think of the living room fireplace where you sit around in your pajamas with loved ones and a good book. I even think of the raging campfire where you find large items (such as a disused pallet or even an abandoned couch) and throw them into a giant heap of flamed goodness. I think that last one might be more for the men reading this.

All of these fires have one thing in common: they are all controlled. They have specific boundaries and limits. In each example, I am in control of the fire, not the other way around. When the fire is in control, it changes everything. No longer are the flames a welcome sight but rather are scary. A fire without limits brings destruction. That which is enjoyable quickly becomes terrifying.

Sex is fire.

When we control sex, with boundaries and limits, it is amazing. When our impulses cause us to remove the boundaries, it is almost unstoppable. It's like starting an uncontrolled fire in a forest next to a group of houses. And destruction follows.

But that sounds so narrow, so limiting! Why can't I enjoy my fire whenever and however I want? How dare someone else assume they have the right to speak into how I make a fire? And how on earth could *limiting* a fire allow me to enjoy it far *more*?

See how the analogy works?

I invite you to pause a moment and reflect on your own life. For those of you with an active sex life, has it been an enjoyable fire or a flaming tornado of destruction? Despite your opinions on the experiences, what do the facts show in your life? Have your relationships been enhanced because of sex or hurt by it?

The healthy boundary for sex is the lifelong commitment of marriage. Sex outside marriage is a forest fire. It often starts like a campfire. It seems controllable, contained, even harmless. I often hear this from couples who plan to marry but see sex ahead of time (usually along with living together) as a logical precursor to their wedding night. But sex doesn't belong with good intentions or a logical plan. That's like choosing to add a container of gas to a campfire because you think you know what you're doing. It doesn't seem that dangerous. Then suddenly the winds shift and you realize the fire has taken over. When sex moves from campfire to forest fire, it will confuse and wound even the strongest among us.

The solution is not to have a better forest fire the next time.

Yet that's precisely what most people do. That's what is normal in our culture. Consider how we justify it.

It was the other person's fault.

It was a fluke.

It won't happen again.

I won't let myself get so attached next time.

It was just the wrong person.

I'll wait longer next time.

The lies we tell ourselves are never ending. The solution is to change the boundaries. That means reserving sex for marriage. It's the only way to get the most out of sex. One of my favorite preachers, Andy Stanley, once asked a woman, "Has sex outside marriage made your life better or just more complicated?" It's a great way of framing the reality we push so hard against.

Many people have become masters of convincing themselves the charred remains of their sexuality are normal and healthy. They aren't.

They aren't normal because that isn't the design. Pastor Tim Liston once said, "Sex outside of marriage hurts a good relationship and prolongs a bad relationship." The results usually speak for themselves if we are willing to honestly look. What does your own track record show?

I know it might sound crazy to you. If you've tried sex outside marriage and you aren't happy with the results, why not try it a different way and see if there is something more to it? What do you have to lose?

If you keep getting burned, it's time to change your view of fire.

BUBBLE GUM SEX

Pornography has moved from a private, guilty pleasure for a small minority of people to an accepted norm of our world today. I've often heard those in my parents' generation talk about how relatively rare it was for them growing up. I even remember my first exposure to porn in junior high. I had to go to a friend's house who had unengaged parents to see the images. I loved every minute of it but had no easy access to it. This would create an on-again-off-again dependence I had with pornography I wouldn't break till I was in college.

Now it is all around me. Lurking in Google search results, in smartphone apps, in my Twitter feed, and in my inbox. I once had to intentionally look to find porn, but now I have to intentionally look not to find it. It terrifies me to think how much access my kids will have.

This is because porn sells. There is no industry need for a porn salesman (can you imagine someone trying to list the "many benefits" of his product?). It sells itself. That collectively our culture is more and more comfortable with it only increases this fact.

If you ask most people today, the prevalent belief is that porn is harmless. If a person uses it alone, it doesn't affect anyone else. Right?

My friend Craig started a ministry called XXXchurch.com. He refers to it as the "Number One Christian Porn Site." They give some sobering statistics on the porn industry today. There are $4.9 billion in sales each year, and 12 percent of websites on the Internet are now porn. That's 4.2 million sites![9]

It isn't just for men anymore either. According to XXXchurch, the breakdown of pornography users is 72 percent male and 28 percent female. And that's for traditional porn avenues that are image based. More on that in a moment.

Porn is an addiction.[10] Anyone who has ever tried to stop after regularly looking at it knows this without a doubt. A recent study from Cambridge University found that brain scans from porn addicts mirror those of drug addicts.[11] Like other addictions, if you continue to look at porn, it takes more and more to satisfy you. Google "the science of pornography addiction" and watch the three-minute video that comes up to see this illustrated.[12] And yes, it's safe to watch at work. This realization of porn as a drug means soft-core porn only works for so long until you get into more intense scenes, relating less and less to what a person might experience in real life. Before a person knows it, they are looking at images that fill them with shame. I've met with people time and again who tell this story.

While you may be content with your involvement with porn at the moment, how far are you willing to go with it? At what point does it shift from "healthy" to unhealthy? For perspective, there are 116,000 searches for child pornography every day.[13] That should turn our stomachs. I doubt these people set out to form an addiction to staring at naked kids. It's the inevitable road of *more* that pornography takes a person down.

> This realization of porn as a drug means soft-core porn only works for so long until you get into more intense scenes, relating less and less to what a person might experience in real life.

This often happens differently for guys and girls, though. While women sometimes view traditional image-based pornography, there are also a variety of ways women deal with a different type of pornography. The difficulty in this discussion is that while image-based porn is usually easy to label, the other variations rarely are.

There is an unhealthy emotional and relational expectation portrayed in so much of our media. Is there really much of a difference in the hyperbolized sexual imagery of typical pornography and the hyperbolized momentary emotional high felt in a romance film or romantic comedy that sends us looking for a "love" that doesn't exist?[14]

I don't need to convince you that men and women behave in dramatically different ways. Ask any married person and they'll provide you with unending examples from their marriage to make this point. This is often true of a couple's sex life. It should come as no surprise that for the typical woman, a temptation for pornography will come less from images of naked people and more from the *feeling* of a graphic love story. This is often known as "emotional porn."

The obvious example might be books like the Fifty Shades of Grey series, but it goes far beyond this. We might consider that series the "hardcore emotional porn," but there are definitely "softcore" versions of it as well. On the other extreme of subtlety, we can even see this manifested in culturally common practices such as Valentine's Day in which we collectively inject steroids into the expectation for a normal relationship. Before you write me off as extreme, consider that the essence of porn is anything that distorts our view of healthy (normal) sex and love.

For the typical woman, emotional porn may be the romance novel (even many of the teen books), the TV show, or the chick flick, each of which stirs up an emotional need for love and then offers a quick fulfillment of it. Have you ever watched a movie about a relationship and thought to yourself that it looked appealing? Maybe it provided something you sensed you currently lack.

While few of us would define our love relationship as perfect, the reason we feel these types of feelings from entertainment like this is because it presents an unrealistic view of love. We sense the disparity of love from onscreen or in the words of our latest page-turner and the love that we actually experience.

This is the same disparity that a man experiences in what a woman seems to be willing to do in the porn industry versus what he actually experiences with women in his own life. Porn in any form provides a fantasy that tempts us to believe as reality. Yet we can never seem to experience that type of reality in our own life. We subconsciously begin to feel our form of reality is actually quite boring compared with what we see from others.

Consider the outcomes of the different types of porn for men and women. When a married man looks at naked images of women, it often negatively affects his ability to find fulfillment in his wife's body (who tends not to look like a porn star). This can alter the way he views her and enjoys her overall. When a married woman connects emotionally to a love story, it often negatively affects her ability to find fulfillment in her husband's romance efforts (who tends not to act like a guy in a chick flick). This can alter the way she views him and enjoys him overall. We might conclude the underlying thread in both of these examples is a fake love that each gender finds appealing, at least in the short term.

This is true even if you aren't married. It will create standards for you that future partners will be unable to meet. And just as some women find traditional porn more appealing, so also some men find emotional porn more appealing. The point is not in the stereotypes but realizing what they all have in common.

Pornography is perhaps the clearest distortion of a pleasure. It takes something good—sex (or the emotional benefits of sex)—and strips it of any of the qualities that make it good. It's all about convenience. It's like eating a diet of only frosting and skipping anything else of nourishment. Sure, it may taste good for a while. But the stomachache, the fatigue, and the poor health will tell a different story in time.

Porn is the bubble gum of sex.

It tastes sweet and gives you something to chew on, but it doesn't fill you up. It can't. Worse yet, it convinces you that you are eating something while you die of starvation. It's like watching a person go from one piece of gum to the next, complaining about their hunger despite their fatigue from chewing. No amount of new gum will fill the craving they have for food. And imagine the paranoia they'll experience if they actually swallow the gum and then have to figure out how many years it will take to digest it!

Contrary to popular belief, most people can digest gum just fine.[15] But gum won't fill you up. The solution is to stop chewing gum and start eating food. So many people have made porn a regular part of their life that the idea of getting rid of it sounds impossible. Even *GQ* magazine, one of those magazines men read "for the articles," recently released ten reasons to stop watching porn.[16] This is the addictive nature of it that nobody wants to talk about.

Here are two links from XXXchurch that may be helpful in this section.

- First, a link to a survey to find out if you have an addiction to porn: http://www.xxxchurch.com/sexual addictiontest.html.

- Second, a link to get help if you are ready to try something else: http://www.xxxchurch.com/help.html.

Like sex outside marriage, if you aren't happy with the results of pornography in your life, why not try life without it and see if you like the results better?

THE ELEPHANT IN THE ROOM

Today, the entire conversation about sex is changing in radically new ways. We have shifted from debating sex outside marriage to debating sex outside a man and woman. On June 27, 2015, the Supreme Court of the United States decided to supercharge the conversation by making it commonplace in all fifty states.

I'll get right to my conclusion here so you can read this next section without trying to guess. I don't believe a same-sex relationship fits the design of a healthy relationship as modeled in the Bible. But my biggest issue with "taking a stand" on this, as people expect many Christians to do, is it alienates the people whom Jesus drew to Himself. To speak out against homosexuality often pushes people who are far from God further from Him, while also increasing the smug satisfaction of many Christians who want nothing to do with gay people.

I want nothing to do with that.

Besides, God doesn't need us to protect Him. He doesn't need us to defend His truth either. Many Christians waste their time fighting cultural battles on behalf of God as if He needs us to rally to His aid. While it might seem this book falls into that category, it certainly isn't my attempt. I'm not writing to defend God but to intrigue you. I'm not worried about God being attacked. I'm worried about Him being overlooked and the fact that we suffer when that happens.

When it comes to homosexuality, I'm not concerned about protecting God. I'm concerned about how to show gay people God loves them and has a design for their life. Since this is a discussion on pleasure, I feel comfortable arguing one point of view. But as to the larger culture war taking place around us, it's time for Christians to concede this one and stop expecting non-Christians to act like Christians. I'm all for equal rights for any marital unions as defined by the government. The Supreme Court's decision affects legal rights, not God's design. We need to be able to see each of them uniquely.

> When it comes to homosexuality, I'm not concerned about protecting God. I'm concerned about how to show gay people God loves them and has a design for their life.

Fear goes a long way in fueling issues like this from people on both sides of the argument. "Don't let them have an inch or they'll take a mile!" That isn't a healthy environment for a person to find his stance. I believe the Bible teaches this isn't what God designed us for, but like the rest of this book, I'm not expecting you to take an argument because the Bible says so.

Let's unpack a few of the logical fallacies we use in discussing homosexuality. A huge part of the problem is our collective inability to discuss this in a healthy way. Often we try to decide where we personally stand on issues like this, but when the conversation turns hostile, it quickly discourages our involvement. Often people either avoid the topic or turn any discussion into a heated debate. Rick Warren wrote,

Our culture has accepted two huge lies. The first is that if you disagree with someone's lifestyle, you must fear or hate them. The second is that to love someone means you agree with everything they believe or do. Both are nonsense. You don't have to compromise convictions to be compassionate.[17]

Warren made his point clearly. We must accept that we can see this from different vantage points and still love one another. Those ideas are not mutually exclusive. Love involves an acceptance of the person, not every action they take or belief they carry. True, they are often linked together. But we must be able to see ourselves as more than any one thing we do or say.

Wherever you land on gay marriage and homosexuality in general, let's put that on the shelf for a moment and discuss whether homosexuality can bring the maximum pleasure from sex. Like we've done elsewhere, we must consider how the Designer's prerogative fits into this discussion.

Were we designed to enjoy sex in this way?

There are plenty of facts and research each side is quick to use for their arguments. Is there or is there not a "gay gene"? As of this writing, nothing has been proven decisively. But it doesn't matter. That's the wrong way of looking at it. We must bring it back to our search for pleasure. Consider this: my wife isn't the only woman I've ever been attracted to. Shocking, right? Does that mean I should pursue another woman the moment I have an inkling of attraction? Absolutely not, even though my body might tell me I am wired for that. The reason I can unabashedly avoid intimate relationships with women other than my wife is that I know it would bring me less pleasure, not more. The pleasure I have in my wife, and in the commitment of our family, far exceeds what I would get in exchange for an affair with another woman. It doesn't matter if a momentary desire tells me otherwise.

This is overly simplified, but the premise rings true elsewhere. Our desires do not equal pleasure necessarily. An alcoholic might recognize a tendency toward drinking to excess, which can shatter his life if pursued the way he wants. Or a man might desire to harm another person in a moment of rage but will hopefully see that this won't produce the ultimate pleasure he's looking for. Indeed, the pleasure of revenge is portrayed to us through entertainment as one of the best pleasures you can experience. The next time you go to a movie, notice how many of the upcoming releases involve a storyline of revenge. But those who pursue revenge usually end up receiving a lot less pleasure than expected.

Whether a man is attracted to other men or whether a woman is attracted to other women is not the issue. The real issue is, can they get the most pleasure by pursuing those types of relationships? Just because it "feels right" in the moment doesn't mean the answer is an obvious yes. This is a tough question for someone to objectively ask themselves, especially when they find they are managing desires that aren't the social norm.

Christians today debate the official biblical stance on gay unions. Many of them weakly cite Old Testament passages out of context to our culture today (remember that prohibition from wearing clothes of mixed fabrics?). To give us a more accurate discussion reference, consider the following three passages from the Bible (each from the New Testament) about homosexuality.

1. "Or do you not know that wrongdoers will not inherit the kingdom of God? Do not be deceived: Neither the sexually immoral nor idolaters nor adulterers nor men who have sex with men nor thieves nor the greedy nor drunkards nor slanderers nor swindlers will inherit the kingdom of God. And that is what some of you were. But you were washed, you were sanctified, you were justified in the name of the Lord Jesus Christ and by the Spirit of our God" (1 Corinthians 6:9–11).

2. "Because of this, God gave them over to shameful lusts. Even their women exchanged natural sexual relations for unnatural ones. In the same way the men also abandoned natural relations with women and were inflamed with lust for one another. Men committed shameful acts with other men, and received in themselves the due penalty for their error" (Romans 1:26–27).

3. "We also know that the law is made not for the righteous but for lawbreakers and rebels, the ungodly and sinful, the unholy and irreligious, for those who kill their fathers or mothers, for murderers, for the sexually immoral, for those practicing homosexuality, for slave traders and liars and perjurers—and for whatever else is contrary to the sound doctrine that conforms to the gospel concerning the glory of the blessed God, which he entrusted to me" (1 Timothy 1:9–11).

Here we see homosexuality addressed in the context of the church by the apostle Paul. We may debate the nuances of the Greek words used (Paul uses the Greek word *malakos* metaphorically in 1 Corinthians 6:9), but most would agree on the message Paul communicated. The question is what to do with those passages.

Now consider this: Jesus never spoke about homosexuality. At least not that we know about. That should cause us to pause for a moment. None of the four guys who wrote detailed accounts of His ministry talked about it. It was certainly around Him at the time, as the apostle Paul addressed it in the three passages above. Jesus certainly spoke about sexual immorality, but usually He was focused more on sex between a couple committed to each other through marriage.

The closest example we have with Jesus occurred when someone asked Him about remarriage. This story appears both in Matthew's and Mark's gospels.[18] Instead of diving into the weeds on the nuances of remarriage, Jesus brought the argument back to God's original design for marriage with a man and a woman as found in the book of Genesis, which goes back to the design for the pleasure of marriage. He referenced the profound metaphor of "one flesh" that God creates when a man and woman unite in covenant commitment together. We are wise to do the same today. No matter what variation of possibilities—other than a man and a woman—we discuss, we stand on stronger ground to go back to the biblical design rather than attempt to easily navigate the complexities of the variations.

And it's only going to get more complex.

It's dangerous to make an argument out of omission, but it's also dangerous to make an argument out of assumption. Despite the fact the word *homosexuality* didn't exist until the nineteenth century,[19] the discussion isn't a new one for our times. History is lined with different examples of it.

While far from exhaustive, I've concluded the biblical intent shows us God's design was for a man and woman to be united in a committed relationship. As my friend Paul Eddy wrote in *Kingdom Sex*,

> The male-female marriage covenant will literally bring forth new human life, thus creating more human beings who will image God in a variety of other types of agape-love relationships. In this sense, the male-female marriage covenant relationship has the capacity to uniquely image the life-producing Triune God.

Sex isn't just a personal or private act. Sex involves our view of God and how we choose to respond to Him. In addition, Christians are called to display Jesus' grace and truth, and many of them have done a terrible job of communicating this to gay people. We tend to want to stand on truth at the expense of grace when it comes to this issue. That's unacceptable.

Most of all, I believe we must be willing to communicate openly without name calling and hate from either side. Love demands a different investment. One where we put aside things that make us uncomfortable if it means the chance to speak grace and truth into someone's life. One where we avoid villainizing people who disagree with us.

It's helpful to remember we are all searching for the same thing even though it manifests itself in different ways. But this topic is far from simple.

THE FLY IN THE BUTTERMILK

My friend Adrian often uses the expression a "fly in the buttermilk." I hate hearing him say this because it means our discussion just got complicated. I think he enjoys saying it to me.

After arguing that a same-sex relationship is not God's design for us, I need to close this chapter by complicating things. We began by looking at God's will, or God's wants. But God doesn't always get what He wants. In fact, He rarely does. This doesn't mean God isn't in control but rather He grants us the ability to make our own decisions.

God doesn't get what He wants every time we sin.

God doesn't get what He wants every time we look for our value from the world.

God doesn't get what He wants whenever we put our faith in ourselves or any other person.

And God doesn't get what He wants every time we choose our own way to find pleasure.

As you might expect, this happens often. God is used to not getting what He wants. But now add God's accommodating will.

This is when God adjusts according to our brokenness. It doesn't mean He changes His standard or His design. Rather, He meets us where we are. Like when God designs a marriage to last a lifetime and then allows a couple to divorce. God acknowledges when we break from a covenant, but it isn't His intent. It's a reflection on us, not on Him.

Sometimes we mess things up so badly that God accommodates

us to help us move forward. This happens when a marriage turns so sour and destructive that the healthiest move a couple can make is to split. It doesn't mean God's plan for marriage had a flaw. It is the result of the individual couple's decisions. Or when God allows two divorced people to get remarried and blesses their union. Again, this was never His intent, yet in that scenario we rarely have such an issue with God giving His blessing anyway. This is why issues like gay marriage should not be given a blanket response. One of the challenges for the church is that we tend to have different standards when it comes to marriage, divorce (for reasons other than abandonment or adultery), and remarriage after such a divorce. When marriage falls short of the biblical view of God's design for relationships, we tend to respond with varying degrees of concern. Many pastors would feel uncomfortable marrying a gay couple but wouldn't hesitate to marry a couple living together or a couple with a divorce or two in their past. I believe the response to all three must be consistent.

Consider this theoretical situation: a gay couple wants to get married as their love for each other is the best part of their lives.

> One of the challenges for the church is that we tend to have different standards when it comes to marriage, divorce … and remarriage after such a divorce … I believe the response to all three must be consistent.

If they are unable to be together, they cannot fathom life. They feel ostracized from most of society but at peace with each other. In fact, they would rather commit suicide than go on living without each other. While this sounds extreme, it sadly isn't far-fetched for some people in this lifestyle.

Is God's will (or design) for them that they would have a gay marriage? From a larger biblical perspective, I believe the answer is no. On a personal level to them, would God rather have them end their lives over this? Absolutely not.

This illustrates the conundrum. Sadly, many gay people conclude they must choose between God and the person they love. Often this is the moment they walk away from God. So it could be possible that in this scenario, God would accommodate their relationship. He may even bless the parts that are pure. The committed love they have for one another might be part of what He blesses.

But all the while He hopes to move them closer to His design. Determining what that means in each situation often feels impossible. What would God want this couple to do? What would God want a gay married couple with four kids to do? There are no easy answers to these questions.

About a year ago I had a longtime friend of mine tell me he's gay. He has been an amazing man of God as long as I've known him. He's worked in a variety of ministry roles over the years. I have always admired the honesty in his pursuit of God and his joy in the process. He exudes a love for others and a selflessness that contagiously draws others to him. This is not a person who does whatever he wants and then justifies it afterward. He's the type of guy who deeply loves Jesus and chooses to follow wherever that leads him.

So I was a bit surprised by his news. Truthfully, it didn't change my view of him as much as it added to the complexity of this topic in my mind.

As he described his journey to my wife and me, he recounted a recent experience he had kissing a man for the first time. He described kissing girls in his life as times when the porch stayed dark. Then he said the first time he kissed a man it was like all the lights in the house came on. For most people reading this, it's a weird thought to consider. It may even trigger a disgust feeling in you. It's hard to relate to the experience as it's foreign to the way most of us feel. But I know the joy of kissing my wife, and I can understand for my friend, that type of feeling only happens with men. For him, the pleasure of a gay relationship far exceeds the pleasure of a straight relationship. He also readily acknowledged the trade off with this as it essentially means giving up the normal life most of us take for granted. Everything from starting his own family, to extended family gatherings, to finding community around him will now look different.

I don't have a way for that to all make sense. I don't think his desires change the design God has for us. But I also don't think he can simply choose something else. He gets a different type of pleasure than most of us do. The only way I can even begin to navigate this type of situation is to acknowledge God's accommodating will is probably bigger than I can even imagine.

On a side note, we should never allow the emotion of disgust to shape our theology or affect the ways we treat others. As an emotion, disgust is absent when we are born and is shaped culturally. It is by no means an authoritative gauge at truth. Yet that is precisely the way most people, Christians included, attempt to navigate homosexuality. It is helpful to remember psychologist Richard Beck's challenge to the church in his book *Unclean*:

What is striking about the gospel accounts is how Jesus reverses negativity dominance. Jesus is, to coin a term, positivity dominant. Contact with Jesus purifies. A missional church embraces this reversal, following Jesus into the world without fears of contamination. But it is important to note that this is a deeply counterintuitive position to take. Nothing in our experience suggests that this should be the case. The missional church will always be swimming against the tide of disgust psychology, always tempted to separate, withdraw, and quarantine.

My friend has spent the last year telling close friends about his sexuality. He ended up doing an impromptu podcast with author and speaker Donald Miller about his story recently, and it turned out to be the catalyst for him to come out publicly.[20] When he originally told my wife and me, he spoke about the grace of God in one of the most moving and powerful ways I've ever heard. He talked about how he knew he needed God's grace before but felt his contributions for God somehow offset this, if even for a little bit. He acknowledged he doesn't want to abuse grace, but that for the first time in his life he soberly sees how badly he needs it.[21] Now he's following after Jesus with that realization in the forefront of his mind. There's something refreshingly honest and beautiful about that.

Or I think back to another person I came in contact with a handful of years ago. I saw I was getting traffic to my blog from a source I was unfamiliar with. After investigating, I realized a clinical psychologist had quoted me on his blog. He also happened to be an openly gay man who had written numerous books on the subject. He cited something from a biblical perspective and used one of my posts as a reference. You see, he was also a Christian.

I e-mailed the psychologist and told him I'd love to start up a conversation on my blog with him to learn more from each other. He jumped at the chance. He was incredibly kind and even wrote out his own journey in six pages. I posted that as well as parts of our conversations on my blog, and we were both encouraged by the majority of comments they received.

In a way, it's surprising to me that the closest two gay people I know are both Christian men. It's not surprising in the sense that I'm probably not often around other gay people who avoid the church whenever possible. But I've learned a lot through these experiences and continue to process all of it. My psychologist friend's perspective challenges the way many Christians assume a gay person thinks. Consider part of what he said to me as he recounted his life:

> I do not understand why God made me gay. I do not understand why God allows people to judge me because I am gay. I don't understand why there was a hurricane in New Orleans, but his lessons for me have been powerful and I trust my faith and my relationship with God above all else. Even the darkest times have brought me growth, insight and a deep faith that there is a reason for everything. I have found that by being true to who I am, I am able to feel more compassion for others, to understand what tolerance and love really mean, and to use my energy for good works. Perhaps God knew all along that he wanted me to share this struggle with you someday or he wanted me to

learn the value of unconditional love and faith. Whatever the reason, I've learned that God is there for me so I don't have to fear the future. Every day is another opportunity to learn and to love.[22]

I don't have an easy way to explain the unique perspectives of my gay friends. But I know that essentially, they want the same things I want. While the specifics change, this is the journey for each of us. You may be quick to pounce on the argument for God accommodating a gay couple, but consider how much accommodation God has made in your life. We each move away from His design, and He works to bring us back. Like I've told my longtime gay friend, we aren't defined by our desires. He's far more than a gay man just as I'm far more than a straight man. We are children of God working to make sense out of God, ourselves, and those around us.

Then there are the stories of gay people who leave that lifestyle. One of the more famous examples is Michael Glatze. Glatze went from being a gay activist, running numerous pro-gay magazines and organizations, to suddenly becoming a Christian who openly spoke out against his previous lifestyle. He said, "It became clear to me, as I really thought about it—and really prayed about it—that homosexuality prevents us from finding our true self within."[23]

This conversation will continue to be in motion. The years to come will continue to produce more examples on all sides of the debate. I pray we continue to search for truth with as much objectivity as we can muster. But that it all takes place on the foundation of love.

HUMBLE HANDS

Of all chapters in this book, this one makes me the most nervous. It's hard to know how culture is limiting the way you see truth. It feels as if this conversation is moving somewhere, and I'm not sure where most of us will land twenty years from now. While that may sound a bit too postmodern for your taste, consider that even some of Jesus' disciples couldn't recognize Jesus when they were talking with Him. After Jesus died and later appeared among His followers, He had an entire conversation with some of them while they walked on the road to Emmaus and didn't realize who He was until later.[24] These were the guys who had just spent three years with Him! How could they not see Him clearly? Yet this concept helps us explain how Christians once argued for slavery and a number of other cultural blemishes throughout history. Applying this text to the spiritual dynamics of homosexuality, Pastor Stan Mitchell argued, "Even the presence of God and a Bible in your lap doesn't give an epiphany."[25]

Truth must be held with humble hands.

Most of all, I'm thankful God doesn't hold His presence from us if we make the wrong choice. When I mess up, when I make a selfish decision, when I fall on my face, God is still with me. Regardless of where a person falls on the specific argument, they can still freely live in the presence and grace of God. We are specifically considering how to live a life of pleasure as designed, not what we do for God to love us.

CHAPTER FIVE

NINE HUNDRED BOTTLES

PURSUING GOD
THROUGH SUBSTANCES

"Do not suppose that abuses are eliminated by destroying
the object which is abused. Men can go wrong with wine
and women. Shall we then prohibit and abolish women?"

Martin Luther

YOU MAY HAVE DETERMINED that the Christian goal is to live as a
monastic teetotaler. Many Christians live as if the Golden Rule says
to avoid alcohol touching your lips. But abstaining from something
just for the *sake* of abstaining is legalism. What I am proposing
is critically examining every pleasure and rightly determining the
way to experience it. This may take you far off the path of what you
heard as a kid or what you have assumed religion teaches.

Like we did with the last chapter on sex, let's take a look at
another specific issue with a lot on the line and one Christians
easily confuse.

Is it wrong to drink alcohol? Specifically, is it wrong to drink to
excess to get drunk?

Like we discussed earlier, what is right is whatever the Designer
determined to maximize the pleasure from it. By looking at some
of the mentions in the Bible about alcohol we can judge the merits

of the instruction. What we'll see here may surprise you. While I don't quote Scripture to create an argument simply about what the Bible says, I've found most people, Christians included, do not have an accurate understanding of the standard the Bible teaches about alcohol.

For those of you who don't normally read the Bible, or haven't ever read it, hang with me. Seeing the biblical perspective is both surprising and intriguing. Once we hear this argument, we can translate it into our own journey toward pleasure today. Consider the following seven passages:

1. "Do not join those who drink too much wine or gorge themselves on meat, for drunkards and gluttons become poor, and drowsiness clothes them in rags" (Proverbs 23:20–21).

2. "Let us behave decently, as in the daytime, not in carousing and drunkenness, not in sexual immorality and debauchery, not in dissension and jealousy. Rather, clothe yourselves with the Lord Jesus Christ, and do not think about how to gratify the desires of the flesh" (Romans 13:13–14).

3. "But now I am writing to you that you must not associate with anyone who claims to be a brother or sister but is sexually immoral or greedy, an idolater or slanderer, a drunkard or swindler. Do not even eat with such people" (1 Corinthians 5:11).

4. "Or do you not know that wrongdoers will not inherit the kingdom of God? Do not be deceived: Neither the sexually immoral nor idolaters nor adulterers nor men

who have sex with men nor thieves nor the greedy nor drunkards nor slanderers nor swindlers will inherit the kingdom of God. And that is what some of you were" (1 Corinthians 6:9–11a).

5. "The acts of the flesh are obvious: sexual immorality, impurity and debauchery; idolatry and witchcraft; hatred, discord, jealousy, fits of rage, selfish ambition, dissensions, factions and envy; drunkenness, orgies, and the like. I warn you, as I did before, that those who live like this will not inherit the kingdom of God" (Galatians 5:19–21).

6. "Therefore do not be foolish, but understand what the Lord's will is. Do not get drunk on wine, which leads to debauchery. Instead, be filled with the Spirit" (Ephesians 5:17–18).

7. "For you have spent enough time in the past doing what pagans choose to do—living in debauchery, lust, drunkenness, orgies, carousing and detestable idolatry" (1 Peter 4:3).

Did you catch what all seven of these passages, from six different books of the Bible, have in common? (The answer is not that they have a lot of fun words in them.)

In each of the passages, the biblical authors teach us to avoid getting drunk, but not to avoid drinking. That's the biblical argument in a nutshell. That's how we experience pleasure with one of the most common substances throughout history. I've met plenty of people who had no idea the Bible even mentioned alcohol in the first place, let alone qualified it.

There's one other passage of note—also from the book of Proverbs—that often creates a bit of confusion for people. At first glance, it may appear this passage communicates a different message.

It is not for kings, Lemuel—it is not for kings to drink wine, not for rulers to crave beer, lest they drink and forget what has been decreed, and deprive all the oppressed of their rights. Let beer be for those who are perishing, wine for those who are in anguish! Let them drink and forget their poverty and remember their misery no more.[1]

The focus here is on Lemuel, not on the perishing people. Seen in that light, this shows the same message. For him to lead well he must avoid the abuses of alcohol. It's quite the stretch to argue that the concession mentioned for those perishing in anguish, poverty, and misery should be the way we choose to use alcohol for pleasure today. Many scholars conclude this latter part refers to offering someone something to take the edge off of dying. This would be more like our modern medicine that we give to a dying person than how much a person should drink on a normal basis.

We even see this discussion popping up in some rather unexpected areas in the first-century church. The following passage is from a letter written by the apostle Paul to the church in Corinth. He reprimanded them because they weren't taking communion the proper way. Communion is when Christians take elements, a form of bread and wine or juice, and remember how Jesus Christ died on the cross for our forgiveness of sins. You might expect Paul was referencing the style in which they took communion, or the frequency of how often they did, or even whom they allowed to take it with them. None of these were the issue.

> So then, when you come together, it is not the Lord's Supper you eat, for when you are eating, some of you go ahead with your own private suppers. As a result, one person remains hungry and another gets drunk.[2]

Paul was mad because they weren't doing it together in a spirit of unity. Some people took so much communion that others had nothing. As a side note, this would have been a full meal, different from most cultural representations of communion in churches today. I can't imagine filling up on the stale wafers I've seen in some churches. But notice the last phrase: some people were using communion to get drunk!

Or another time, a day famously known as Pentecost, onlookers accused the apostles of drunkenness since they were each speaking different languages. The apostle Peter gave the defense for his crew, and I love his argument: "These people are not drunk, as you suppose. It's only nine in the morning!"[3]

He didn't say, "These people are not drunk, as you suppose. We have never drank alcohol!"

He didn't say, "These people are not drunk, as you suppose. We gave all that up when we followed Jesus."

He didn't say, "These people are not drunk, as you suppose. We don't drink, smoke, or chew, or go with women who do."

Rather, Peter's argument was that it was too early in the morning to drink! In effect Peter said, "Seriously, at 9:00 a.m.?"

One time I was at a Christian conference[4] in Nashville. Part of the three-day experience involved picking what they called a "learning community" for Friday morning of that week. Keep in mind this particular conference was all about mixing church and culture and seeing things in a fresh way. My group selected a class called "The Tradition of Whiskey." It was scheduled from ten in the morning till noon. We figured it was a class about whiskey but not necessarily involving whiskey.

We were wrong.

Turns out I had the unique opportunity to experience a whiskey tasting at ten in the morning. I can relate to Peter's argument. At one point our instructor asked us to put our nose in our glass and then asked the question, "What does this smell like to you?"

Without skipping a beat my friend replied, "Broken dreams."

To her credit, the instructor was ready with her own witty reply. She looked over at my friend and asked, "What was her name?"

Weird things happen when you try to drink in the morning. It's the unwritten rule of enjoying alcohol for most people. That's why we have jokes about it being "five o'clock somewhere."

Alcohol isn't a new source of pleasure for us to ponder today. In fact, in Tom Standage's book *The History of the World in Six Glasses*, he told the history of civilization through the dominant drink in each time period. He put them in this order: beer, wine, hard spirits, tea, coffee, and cola. Notice the first three of the six are alcoholic! And it didn't take us too long to find ways to add alcohol to the last three as well.

As a result, we are fortunate the Bible specifically addresses this topic that is just as relevant today, if not more so. In fact, while avoiding any instruction to completely avoid alcohol, there is a passage where the apostle Paul recommended that one of his apprentices actually start drinking. He encouraged Timothy to "stop drinking only water, and use a little wine because of your stomach and your frequent illnesses."[5]

> If you don't want to drink alcohol based on your personal preferences, that is fine ...
> But don't credit it to a biblical mandate.

You don't have to avoid drinking from a supposed spiritual mandate. Pleasure in alcohol comes from enjoying it without drinking to the point it causes us to be drunk. If you don't want to drink alcohol based on your personal preferences, that is fine. Because of your past experiences, it may be more pleasurable for you to avoid it completely. But don't credit it to a biblical mandate. It helps to consider the way in which C. S. Lewis addressed the subject of alcohol in his book *Mere Christianity*.

Of course it may be the duty of a particular Christian, or of any Christian, at a particular time, to abstain from strong drink . . . But the whole point is that he is abstaining, for a good reason, from something which he does not condemn and which he likes to see other people enjoying. One of the marks of a certain type of bad man is that he cannot give up a thing himself without wanting every one else to give it up. That is not the Christian way.

Pleasure lives in the balance. This idea also has another name that unfortunately doesn't have much excitement around it. Moderation.

MODERATION: A LONG FOUR-LETTER WORD

Am I really suggesting a person should willingly stop drinking after two or three drinks? Depending on your social life, this is literally a buzzkill of a notion. The problem is we tend not to see drunk people on commercials for alcohol. If we formed opinions of what is was like to drink alcohol purely based on advertisements, we'd likely not even know that it was possible to get drunk. It's almost as if these companies know they can sell you on moderation, but anything beyond that won't sell for obvious reasons. So we don't talk about that part publicly, and they wink to us in the commercial as we watch all those people having a good time. You can sell a variety of other products by showing these same people the next morning!

I recently spoke at a friend's church in New Jersey and brought my wife with me. Michelle and I stayed an extra couple of days in New York after I was done. One of the nights we paid to do a five-hour tour of the city. In our group were four girls from Canada on a bachelorette party. Our tour ended around 11:00 p.m., but I overheard the girls talking about going to a strip club to party afterward. Before you judge me for listening in, they weren't exactly discreet about it. They began asking the girl who was getting married what kind of alcohol she wanted to get drunk on. Much to my surprise, she replied that she didn't want to get drunk at all. She started to explain how it gives her a headache, a stomachache, and makes her feel awful. Instead of being supportive of their friend, and the reason these girls made a trip out of the country, one of the girls mocked her for sounding like a Pepto-Bismol commercial! To be fair, she *was* doing hand motions while she protested what alcohol would do to her.

How could moderation possibly be a more pleasurable way to

enjoy alcohol? Let's unpack this. Don't get drunk. Why? Because it doesn't produce a life of pleasure. Martin Luther once described drunkenness as "when the tongue walks on stilts and reason goes forward under half a sail." It isn't a good place to be. Like sex outside marriage, the lack of pleasure the consequences bring outweighs the immediate pleasure. I'm amazed whenever I hear on the news about another celebrity who screwed up their life with a DUI. These are people who appear to have everything yet lose much of it because of the consequences of how they use alcohol.

As I've mentioned, I'm a huge baseball fan. Our local team is the Arizona Diamondbacks. Recently, one of the two broadcasters was a former player named Mark Grace. He and Pete Rose are the only two players to lead a decade in most hits yet not be named to the Hall of Fame. Mark Grace had a distinguished career on the field and has since had a distinguished career in broadcasting after his retirement. But after two DUI arrests in fifteen months, Mark Grace lost his job as Diamondbacks commentator.

Why? Because something he used for pleasure turned to rob him of pleasure. This is the deception of pleasure in real-world examples we see so often we hardly even notice. I challenge you right now to think of a high-profile person who has had their life derailed because of alcohol. I bet you can do it without breaking a sweat. We know the devastating power alcohol often brings.

In a more immediate sense, how anyone could experience a hangover in the morning and then have the desire to go back to drinking that night is beyond me. Just consider the stories people tell about vomiting, blacking out, or having no memory of what happened hours prior. And then they get to reflect on all of this the next day with an immense headache to boot. These are far from enjoyable experiences, but many assume it comes with the territory.

Alcohol in moderation is a pleasure without any of those detractors. Logic dictates the pleasure of alcohol without all of those consequences is far greater than the pleasure of alcohol with them.

But it goes beyond that.

Consider the experience of drinking for an alcoholic. I've had plenty of friends who would consider themselves recovering alcoholics. The not-so-pleasurable side of alcohol burned them in the past and they have no desire to repeat it. Many of them avoid drinking completely because they know what will happen if they do. Others will ask me to help them drink in moderation. But their experience is far less enjoyable than mine. They might savor the taste of their drink more than I do, but they also have a fear in the back of their mind of what could happen. Or they have all the associations and memories of bad experiences with alcohol stirring up from the bottom of their glass.

I have none of that. I've never abused alcohol in this way. I have no negative memories or associations with it. I can enjoy a drink or two at a time without anything else looming over my shoulder. That's pleasure.

Anyone who chooses the alternative is accepting the cultural norm at the expense of the logic of the biblical narrative. Author Stephen Mansfield wrote in *The Search for God and Guinness*,

Many historians have noted that this positive Christian perspective on alcohol probably even encouraged brewing, because it both sanctioned a temperate love of beer and welcomed beer as an alternative to more high-alcohol drinks. This theory is supported by the fact that beer is so intertwined with the history of the Christian faith that it is tempting to believe that Christians discovered it. Perhaps in its holy and moderate use, they did.

DID JESUS DRINK?

Like the seven passages we saw at the beginning of this chapter, answering the question of whether Jesus Himself drank alcohol will likely surprise many people.

Regardless of whether you believe in Jesus or just think He was a historical person, you are likely familiar with His reputation for doing miracles. Events like walking on water, raising people from the dead, and casting out demons, to name just a few.

But did you know Jesus' first miracle happened at a party?

Here is the way it played out as recorded in the second chapter of the gospel of John. Jesus was at a wedding reception with His disciples and his mother. At some point in the celebration they ran out of wine. Now it doesn't matter if the year is AD 30 or AD 2000; running out of drinks at a party is never a good thing. This spelled disaster for the newly united couple and their reputations among this close-knit community.

But then an odd thing happened.

Jesus' mother came to Him and pointed out there wasn't any more wine. This is like when my wife tells me *we* need to take out the trash. What she is really saying is that *I* need to stop what I'm doing and take out the trash. Jesus' mother was essentially prodding Him to bend the laws of nature. (Subtly more impressive than when I take out the trash).

He didn't bite. Instead, He responded by telling her His time hadn't yet come. He hadn't officially done a miracle yet and wasn't sure this was the right time to begin. She ignored this and told the servants to do whatever her son told them.

Even Jesus wasn't immune from the mom effect.

Jesus knew the gravity of the moment. If He did something now, the expectations would begin: the crowds, the pressure, the persecution. All of it hung on this unusual moment.

Around them were six jars able to hold twenty to thirty gallons of liquid each. Jesus instructed the servants to fill them with water. Then He told the servants to serve the liquid to one of the leaders of the party. After tasting the water that had now become wine, he pulled the groom aside and expressed his amazement that he would save the best wine for last!

That meant Jesus made a hundred and eighty gallons of wine for party-goers who had already drunk everything reserved for the party. On average, a gallon of wine equals five bottles.

So Jesus made roughly *nine hundred bottles* of wine for the party! Not just that, but nine hundred bottles of unbelievably good wine.

Stop to think about the scene. The people at the party had already drunk all the planners thought was necessary. And then Jesus produced *more* alcohol.

This produces some tricky questions to consider.

Did people get drunk on the wine Jesus made?

Was Jesus drinking His own wine?

Regardless of what you do with some of the bigger implications of this story, Jesus' first miracle shows us He didn't have the aversion to alcohol many people assume He did.

The countdown to the cross began with alcohol.

There's another passage that gives us insight into Jesus' involvement with alcohol. The gospel of Matthew records a conversation where Jesus compared Himself to one of His early followers named John the Baptist. Jesus was talking to a group of religious leaders who were angry with both John and Jesus. So Jesus saw an opportunity to make a point.

> For John came neither eating nor drinking, and they say, "He has a demon." The Son of Man came eating and drinking, and they say, "Here is a glutton and a drunkard, a friend of tax collectors and sinners." But wisdom is proved right by her deeds.[6]

In this passage we learn some people accused Jesus of being a drunkard. What does that tell us? It at least means He drank regularly enough for people to see. If we look at the context of the argument He made, we can also assume this accusation of Jesus being a drunkard didn't have evidence to support it.

Jesus' point was that John the Baptist didn't drink alcohol and people said he had a demon, while Jesus did drink alcohol and people said He was a drunkard. These people were looking to create faults in anything. John didn't have a demon, and Jesus wasn't a drunk. But the fact they could even accuse Him shows us He likely drank.

Both of these passages show that Jesus didn't avoid wine nor did He preach against it. But there is also no indication He abused it either. It continues the theme we've seen elsewhere.

A study of the history of the church reveals that great spiritual leaders have followed this example. The idea of enjoying alcohol through moderation has a long history in the church.

Consider just a few examples to make this point starting with the Pilgrims. They are a staple of American history in their pursuit for religious freedom. As much as it may come as a surprise, the Pilgrims also brought with them a dependence on beer, according to *The Search for God and Guinness.*

> Their critical shortage made a brewhouse a priority among the structures built that first winter in Plymouth. Even if the Pilgrims' supply weren't scarce, the need for a brewery was immediate. The population of the small colony expanded faster than ale could be shipped from Europe. And of all the hardships the settlers endured, the lack of beer caused them the most displeasure.[7]

Mansfield also writes that the fiery preacher Jonathan Edwards was "famous among his friends for nursing a glass of punch throughout an evening with family or while preparing his sermons at night." In his *Institutes of the Christian Religion,* John Calvin said, "It is permissible to use wine not only for necessity, but also to make us merry." The renowned preacher George Whitefield once wrote, "Give my thanks to that friendly brewer for the keg of rum he sent us."

Martin Luther is another key figure we have for an example. According to *The Story of Civilization: The Reformation,* during the time of Luther, "a gallon of beer per day was the usual allowance per person, even for nuns." Luther's wife, Katie, was a skilled brewer. Luther even incorporated humor into his defense of drinking.

He said, "If God can forgive me for having crucified Him with Masses twenty years running, He can also bear with me for occasionally taking a good drink to honor Him."

Even if we look at those on the alcohol side of history, we see a surprising connection to faith. Arthur Guinness, who created the beer company with his name, set up the first Sunday schools in Ireland, challenged the practice of dueling, and chaired the board of a hospital for the poor. His grandson, Henry Grattan Guinness, was such a powerful Christian leader of his day he was ranked with Dwight L. Moody and Charles Spurgeon. Some have referred to him as the Billy Graham of the nineteenth century.

> A study of the history of the church reveals that great spiritual leaders have followed this example. The idea of enjoying alcohol through moderation has a long history in the church.

Moderation is a skill in which Christian leaders have excelled. This is worth celebrating and remembering today for the pleasure to be found in it. Avoid getting drunk, but you don't have to avoid drinking.

THINGS YOU CAN SMOKE IN A PIPE

Usually after a conversation about the biblical perspective on alcohol someone will say something to this effect: "Yeah, but the Bible doesn't say anything about marijuana!" You can exchange the last word in that sentence for just about anything you can smoke in a pipe, and some other drugs you can't. This conversation is growing now that some states have legalized marijuana.

The passages and context about alcohol in this chapter can

easily apply to other types of drugs as well. It may come as a surprise that the Bible doesn't directly mention Ecstasy or smoking weed, but that doesn't mean we need to throw up our hands in indecision.

Like alcohol, people often find immediate pleasure with drugs at the cost of a greater pleasure later. The motive for the typical person's drug use is often to numb themselves or experience a release from normal life. As Epicurus put it, "The limit of the extent of pleasure is the removal of all pain." Drugs go a long way for people to remove the pain that is overwhelming them.

But the release is short-sighted. What may bring immediate relief also brings new problems, as any addict or close friend or family member of an addict can testify.

The equivalent can occur with a drunk person, who is no longer in control of themselves. They have allowed a substance to override their own reason and intuition. In a way, they remove themselves from the present moment. Any substance used to reach the same effect as drunkenness, regardless of how it specifically impairs a person, is equally as limiting to pleasure. We accept greater consequences that decrease our overall pleasure for a smaller, momentary pleasure.

What about tobacco? Smoking tobacco does not impair a person like drunkenness, yet some Christians have been just as dogmatic against it as they have alcohol.

But here the conversation is surprisingly simple and straightforward. We can apply the same conclusion we saw with the biblical view on alcohol. Since tobacco does not provide the same impairment as an excess of alcohol or other types of drugs, it fits within the plan for pleasure.

Here we enter subjective waters that quickly create disagreement. Smoking a pipe or a cigar is no different from having a drink or two in moderation. Cigarettes, especially these days, have a negative connotation, but this hasn't always been the case (even Andy Griffith and Curious George's owner smoked). Now we all would agree that tobacco is bad for your health.

But so is super-sizing your meal,

not getting enough sleep,

not exercising regularly,

drinking soda,

and driving an SUV that heavily pollutes the air.

Yet I've heard few (if any) sermons preaching against those sins. The health concern is not the real argument, even though many people make it appear that way. Our real argument is how we can maximize our pleasure.

Like we saw with a history of alcohol, Christian leaders throughout the years have enjoyed tobacco as well. C. S. Lewis used to smoke in a room until he turned it into "a proper fug." The great preacher R. W. Dale smoked so regularly his son said, "Food and drink he could forego without a pang, but cut off from tobacco, he was little better than a lost soul." Campbell Morgan was rumored to smoke eight cigars a day.

A Methodist preacher once challenged Charles Haddon Spurgeon about his smoking. Spurgeon promised him, "If I ever find myself smoking to excess, I promise I shall quit entirely." Sounds like a good answer. But the man asked him to clarify what he meant by excess.

Spurgeon replied, "Why, smoking two cigars at the same time!"

The great preacher Philip Brooks described his ideal vacation as "plenty of books and time and tobacco." A friend described the minister turned journalist William Robertson Nicoll this way: "It was weird to watch him as he lay there, amid a medley of newspapers and books and pipes and cigarettes ashes, and to know that his brain was busy absorbing knowledge and incubating ideas all the time."[8]

Moderation isn't as bad as it sounds. Christians have been championing this idea for hundreds of years. That's why it's time for us to revisit it today in our search for pleasure.

We can then apply this moderation principle to whatever drug popularizes the culture we live in. Again, this takes common sense and some objectivity. A friend of mine recently argued to me he could smoke weed in moderation (without being impaired). While I doubt the logic of his argument, it presents an interesting case. I'm sure we'll develop more drugs in the years to come that may fall into this gray category. Without creating a specific list—which would quickly become outdated—we instead should logically stand firm on not trading long-term pleasure for a momentary impairment. That tradeoff will always end with less pleasure overall. When it comes to substances, moderation is the key to lasting pleasure.

CHAPTER SIX

HEAVY LIFTING

PURSUING GOD
THROUGH WORK

"Being good at anything is like figure skating—
the definition of being good at it is being able
to make it look easy. But it never is easy."

Hugh Macleod

NEARLY EVERY PERSON ON THIS PLANET has experience with the concept of work. Work causes us to focus on delayed gratification, and that's the reason why many people dread it or, at the very least, tolerate it. The other reason we feel so negatively about work is that we often spend the majority of our time working in areas we do not enjoy. That's why so many people feel a sense of dread and loathing every Sunday night in anticipation of Monday morning.

But is work itself really to blame?

We need to redefine our definition of work to get to the answer. For many of us, work equates to doing something we have to do but don't want to do. Sometimes we define it as manual labor or something similar. I submit those are awful definitions. The dictionary defines *work* as "exertion or effort directed to produce or accomplish something."[1]

I'd define work as that in which we spend our energy to see

results. With that definition, we can include traditional applications such as yard work or a nine-to-five job. But it also includes the efforts of a stay-at-home mother or a hobbyist looking to do more with his passion.

Here again, the Bible shows us a fascinating insight. In Genesis—the first book of the Bible—chapter 3 unpacks Adam and Eve's disobedience. We looked at that earlier. But a chapter before shows us something we might not expect. After God created a paradise for humanity to live in, "the LORD God took the man and put him into the Garden of Eden to work it and take care of it."[2] God put Adam to work. Someone had to prune and water paradise so God assigned those jobs to Adam. In today's terms we might classify this as blue-collar work. Depending on where you live in the world, you likely have varying experiences with tending nature. I've had experience planting and mowing grass along with planting and trimming trees and bushes. That's about it. So I'll be honest, the thought of taking care of the utopian garden of Eden sounds a bit intense to me! No pressure there.

God also tasked Adam with naming all of the new animals God had just thought up.[3] That might not sound like a big deal at first, but consider your last visit to the zoo as a launching pad for the diversity and sheer volume of this assignment. I can only imagine him carrying his Moleskine notebook while he walked around coming up with names of what to call the life forms around him. And you thought you dealt with writer's block! Adam was the world's first biologist. In today's terms we might classify this job as white-collar.

God tells Adam to take care of the garden and name the animals. His work included both blue-collar and white-collar assignments. This was easily a forty-plus-hours-a-week occupation to keep him busy. So why does all this matter?

Genesis shows us work is part of paradise.

Life changed for the worse for Adam, Eve, and their descendants after God kicked them out of the garden of Eden. But the concept of work wasn't a new part of that punishment. Work existed *in* the garden. But now Adam's work would be more difficult as a result: "The LORD God banished him from the Garden of Eden to work the ground from which he had been taken."[4] He still had work to do, but now instead of the lush vegetation of the garden of Eden, Adam had to cultivate a new soil.

> It will produce thorns and thistles for you;
>> and you will eat the plants of the field.
> By the sweat of your brow
>> you will eat your food
> until you return to the ground.[5]

Here enters the basis for the misunderstanding many people carry with them today. When work involves sweat and thorns and thistles, how could it possibly be anything enjoyable? Yet at the heart of work—when we apply ourselves to a result—is pleasure. It's also something we see God Himself do in the first pages of the Bible.

Consider it logically. There's nothing quite like the good night's sleep you have after a long day of any type of work. You sleep well from the exhaustion of having spent yourself. By contrast, have you ever had a lazy day and taken a late-afternoon nap and then tried to go to sleep at your normal time? If you're like me, it often means staring at the ceiling and quite a bit of tossing and turning. I'd rather go to bed tired than go to bed rested any night. Ironically, waking up rested often depends on going to sleep tired. Said another way, going to sleep rested negates waking up rested.

Or have you ever caught yourself basking in satisfaction over results you've achieved? Whether it's staring at a freshly cut front lawn, watching your kids have a moment of selflessness for another, driving your car after you changed the oil yourself, or reading through last quarter's record numbers, seeing the results of your effort is a powerful pleasure. I've even caught myself doing this with an empty sink after cleaning the dishes. Okay, I do that every time I wash the dishes.

> Your day job has as much potential for pleasure as your dream job … The best way to get there is to find pleasure in your job now.

Work done right provides pleasure during and after.

For many people, the closest they get to the idea of work and pleasure is some far-off concept of a dream job. Sure, I could get paid to do *that*, then I'd have work with pleasure. We banish work out from the garden and accept our doomed fate. But they aren't mutually exclusive. Jon Acuff wrote in *Quitter*,

> That's the biggest reason it's critical you work hard at your day job. You're not just working; you're practicing for your dream. Even if they're completely unrelated, and I'm not sure they are, the effort you invest in work will return big dividends to your dream. If you want your dream job to work, work on your day job.

Your day job has as much potential for pleasure as your dream job. Even if you remain convinced your dream job would be substantially better, the best way to get there is to find pleasure in your job now. Work was designed to be part of paradise. As even Aristotle acknowledged, "Pleasure in the job puts perfection in the work."

Not to be a downer, but if there was work in the garden of Eden, that also means there will be work in heaven! Wait, you were thinking of heaven as a resort? Don't worry; we'll all have our dream jobs. I'm pretty sure I'll be some type of cheese chef.

ONE MARSHMALLOW OR TWO?

We live in a culture of instant. Instant coffee, instant oatmeal, instant pudding, instant beans, instant potatoes, instant rice, instant stuffing, instant everything. When it comes to food, most people want it hot and fresh and quick. We live in a time in history where this is readily available for most of the developed world.

I love technology. Specifically, I love the convenience and speed at which technology allows me to live. I can reload my Starbucks card using the Starbucks app on my iPhone while I wait in line for my iced, venti, eight-pump vanilla, iced coffee with cream. From my bank account to my phone to my mouth.

Seamless.

Remember the old days, when you had to carry cash, and then manually have an employee reload the cash onto a gift card (which you had to pick out from a store), and then you had to make sure you had enough cash on you or enough on your gift card at all times? Phew, what a bummer.

Not anymore.

We thrive on immediate gratification. If I can benefit right now, then I'm in. My Starbucks app on my phone automatically loads more money onto it when my balance gets low. That's immediate, and doesn't even require anything from me. Want to make a lot of money? Find a way to give people something good the moment they buy it. Want to work on your selling skills? Convince people what you are selling is so good it will be worth their wait from the time they buy it till the time they get to enjoy it. Immediate gratification always outsells delayed gratification.

But delayed gratification usually brings better results in the long term. Delayed gratification requires us to consider the bigger picture of what we want, not just what we want in the moment.

I remember watching a simple video of an experiment with kids.[6] With cameras rolling, they sat a single giant marshmallow in front of each child. The instructions were simple. If the child could wait until the instructor came back without eating his marshmallow, he would get a second marshmallow to eat. Or he could eat one marshmallow now.

Then the instructor walked out, and we watch the agony on the faces of these sweet children as they wrestle with their decision. It is downright hilarious.

Most of them wait. But not before they smell, lick, and nibble all around that one marshmallow. The wait almost looks painful for some of them. But the complete joy on the faces of the kids who make it through the waiting period proves the wait was worth it. They celebrate their two marshmallows like Willy Wonka just invited them to hang out with the Oompa Loompas at the factory. Their struggle was not in vain. Google "the marshmallow test" and you can watch it for yourself.

It doesn't get any easier when we grow up.

We experience our own marshmallow test daily. But since our test isn't as obvious, we usually have no idea we are making a critical decision in the moments that make up each day. Our brain often works against us as it judges the moment instead of the bigger picture. Consider the last time you received difficult feedback from someone you respect. Everything inside you likely wanted to find a way to make it stop at all costs. You could write them off, defend yourself, or just run out of the room. Yet you knew that if you pushed through the momentary discomfort of hearing the feedback, you could grow and develop into more later. The momentary discomfort was a piece of the journey to a bigger pleasure.

> Delayed gratification isn't sexy. But it is a key part of living a life of pleasure. Delayed gratification separates the true pleasure seeker from the hobbyist.

It's the difference between a person passing up the immediate pleasure of a bag of greasy food for a healthy cooked meal at home.

It's the difference between a person passing up the immediate pleasure of relaxation for the physical benefits of working out.

It's the difference between a person passing up the immediate pleasure of sex with a stranger for a better sex life through marriage.

It's the difference between a person passing up the immediate pleasure of a quick fix so they don't deal with the larger shackles of addiction.

Delayed gratification isn't sexy. But it is a key part of living a life of pleasure. Delayed gratification separates the true pleasure seeker from the hobbyist. Only the person on the bigger journey with the end in mind has the insight and discipline to choose that which brings the greatest pleasure.

Few great pleasures happen immediately. That's why work, or that in which we spend our energy to see results, tends to be so hard for so many people. Results take time. And the bigger the results desired, usually the more work involved up front.

In writing, it's the difference between blogging and writing a book. If I write a post on my blog, I get instant feedback through shares and comments. It's great. When I write content for a book, it's usually months or years before most people will read it. It takes a totally different motivation. But it's also the difference between holding your own book in your hand versus seeing the link to your latest post. They both give me a sense of satisfaction, but they don't even compare on the magnitude.

What pleasure in the results are you missing out on because of an avoidance of work? Can you imagine holding your own book in your hand? What about a music album or a video you made? Maybe it's a new business or nonprofit that you bring into creation. I'm convinced that most people have God-given passions in them that will only come to existence through a pursuit of pleasure in our work. It won't always be easy, and much of it will take time, but there are immense amounts of pleasure to be found in work.

Not to mention from a purely logical point of view, most of us spend the majority of our week at a physical job. If you conclude the pleasure part of your day doesn't start till 5:00 p.m., you've effectively thrown out a majority of your opportunities. Instead, we can find pleasure in the work itself and the delayed results we can experience through it.

KEYFRAMES VS. INBETWEENS

What happens when you oust a guy as brilliant as Steve Jobs from Apple, the company he created? You get the other companies he starts, like Pixar, which is equally renowned for its creativity and ability to change the status quo. And you end up finding a way to bring Steve Jobs back to Apple.

Those of us not involved in this staffing debacle can celebrate what this awkward lapse produced. Pixar caused the decades-old industry of animation to take on radically new looks. It changed the game. We'd seen cartoon characters like this before, but with movies like *Toy Story* in 1995, we saw what a full feature-length movie looks like using computer animation.

One of the intriguing parts of Pixar's computer technology involves something they call "keyframes." These are the key moments in the action that the computer later connects together using "inbetweens." Essentially, artists animate a few key moments for each scene and then allow the computer to animate the details between each key moment. This allows animators to avoid having to create every frame in painstaking detail.

It's actually just adding computers to the process people already used. In traditional animation, the senior artist would draw the keyframes and then her assistant would animate the inbetweens by hand. The inbetweens have always been a necessary evil for animators, usually reserved for those with less seniority. The inbetweens don't define or guide the scene. Rather, they allow the scene to make sense to our eyes as we see the bigger picture happening between the keyframe moments. If we listen to animators describe using both computer and traditional animation, we find that with computer animation, an animator needs less keyframes.[7] We might say that's the goal of a good animation software: automate more of the inbetweens so fewer keyframes are needed. The animator's job gets easier as the computer owns more and more of the details of the inbetweens.

In animation, we start with keyframes that shape the inbetweens. But with our pleasures, the opposite is true. We start with inbetweens that shape our keyframes. The problem is many people fail to see this contrast and approach their pleasures like an animator with a cartoon.

One of the reasons we struggle in our understanding of pleasure is we often approach it from a keyframe point of view. We think pleasure is what happens in the highlight reel moments and the rest is just the necessary details to get there. We might think, *I work so I can party. The two share nothing else in common.* Yet this keeps us from seeing that *how* our pleasure keyframes connect determines *what* our keyframe moments ultimately become.

Instead, if we approach pleasure from an inbetween point of view, we begin to see how everything connects together and why it matters. Like in animation, this is tempting to delegate to someone or something else. While there will never be a computer equipped to do this for us, there are plenty of people who will gladly decide this for us. Friends and influencers all around us will encourage us to focus on the keyframes and trust their advice for the inbetweens. After all, that's what we naturally want to do anyway.

If we're honest, the inbetween moments can be tedious. They are the moments most people will never see. But these are the moments that provide the environment for our character to develop.

Every now and then I'll find a great truth in an unexpected

place. Since I believe all truth anywhere belongs to God, I'm constantly trying to be open to unexpected sources. Even Ashton Kutcher chick flicks. In the 2003 movie *Just Married*, Kutcher's character, Tom, experiences the extreme highs and lows of marriage all within a short amount of time. During one of the scenes in which Tom considers giving up on the marriage, he receives some shockingly good advice from his dad.

> Mr. Leezak: Some days your mother and me loved each other. Other days we had to work at it. You never see the hard days in a photo album . . . but those are the ones that get you from one happy snapshot to the next.

This idea of the unseen hard days that get us from one happy snapshot to the next is a tremendous metaphor for inbetweens. While these moments don't make it into the photo album of our life (that's for the keyframes), they connect one photo to the next. As Mr. Leezak coached his son in the movie, we must learn to focus on those moments instead of the more public ones only.

We approach our inbetweens well whenever we

- forego a momentary pleasure for something we're looking ahead to;
- invest ourselves into something bigger than the current moment;
- save ourselves for something bigger than the current moment; or
- live this moment with the sole purpose to build up to a keyframe later (practice delayed gratification).

Unlike animation, our goal is not less keyframes, but more. In fact, we want to get to the place where our keyframes and our inbetweens are harder to distinguish between. When we delegate the details of our pleasure, we submit to the mercy of other people's ideas for what our pleasure eventually becomes.

You own your pleasure inbetweens, not just your pleasure keyframes. These should never be delegated. Unlike animation, they cannot be separated without dramatically altering the end result. Yet we are short-sighted to only focus on the keyframes, the moments we celebrate and talk about with our friends (for example, the stereotypical weekend in Vegas). While your keyframe pleasure moments will be the ones to make it to your social media outlets, they won't be the ones to determine how enjoyable your pleasures will be.

You can find pleasure and a deeper sense of fulfillment even if you are staring face-to-face at a "case of the Mondays." Work makes for an easy target, but anyone interested in a life of pleasure learns to see beyond that. The highs and lows of the journey offer joys that mere happiness could never compete with.

CHAPTER SEVEN

TO LOVE A RATTLESNAKE

PURSUING GOD
THROUGH PARENTING

"A child is conceived in ecstasy but birthed with much pain."

Joel A. Freeman

Choosing to have kids often begins with a husband and wife wanting a family. They wish to experience a new type of love. They want to expand their community of their immediate home. But the new parents quickly realize that after that first baby cry, parenting is no longer about *their* needs. True, some parents still take longer than others to make this transition. Some never do. I recently heard a mom explain she intentionally became pregnant (outside of marriage) because she wanted a friend. That's an awful reason to have a child. And a bad way to look for pleasure.

That's because parenting demands something from a person unlike anything else. My friend describes it as choosing to love a rattlesnake. I've lost count of the amount of times I've been peed on or thrown up on. How many times I've been woken up in the middle of the night. How many naps I wished for but never had. How many of my things have been broken by their little fingers (some of my childhood toys survived three decades only to be dismembered by a four-year-old). Or how many times we were wrestling and they chose to kick Daddy in a certain area while I was defenseless. And that's just this week!

And this is the point. If I saw a rattlesnake in front of me on a path, I would stop and turn around or go far around it. I wouldn't choose to interact with it because I know the pain and harm that would bring. Yet with parenting, we choose it fully knowing (or at least with a suspicion of) what it will cost us.

Because I have four kids, I'm often asked by future parents what to expect. My answer: it will be harder than anything you've ever done, but it will be more fulfilling than anything you've done. It will provide a pleasure unlike anything else you'll find elsewhere.

But that pleasure is expensive (both literally and figuratively).

> The more kids you have, the more variations of your own personality you get to see.

If we poll the typical person on their views of parenting we can find out a lot about their pursuit of pleasure. Some people know that kids would limit what they want to do—usually travel or career goals—so they intentionally decide not to ever have them. Most common are parents who will have one or two. This is usually seen as "reasonable" or what they "can afford." They want the pleasure of kids, but they also know the limit of what they can give. Then you have the crazy parents like Michelle and me who are suckers for punishment (we might still have more kids). I defend our family of six by explaining that chaos plus chaos is still just chaos.

Parents know that kids bring out something unique in them as they rise to the challenge of raising their children. This is part of the pleasure of parenting, even though we often don't think of it in this way. As the comedian Jim Gaffigan argued in his book *Dad Is Fat*:

> I guess the reasons against having more children always seem uninspiring and superficial. What exactly am I missing out on? Money? A few more hours of sleep? A more peaceful meal? More hair? These are nothing compared to what I get from these five monsters who rule my life. I believe each of my five children has made me a better man. So I figure I only need another thirty-four kids to be a pretty decent guy.

I love telling stories about my kids. I love the variety of their personalities. The more kids you have, the more variations of your own personality you get to see. I love the way I interact uniquely with each one. Recently our second child, Madsen, came downstairs at 11:30 p.m. He couldn't sleep. Silently he walked into the living room where Michelle and I were sitting and grabbed a magnetic writing board. Then he went back upstairs to his room. He didn't utter a word to us.

Later, I went in to check on him. I cracked his door open slightly and stared at his bed, waiting for my eyes to adjust. The room was too dark for me to see him clearly on his bed. After about a minute, I heard from the dark, "What are you doing." Notice I didn't include a question mark in his statement. That's because he said it in an eerily monotone voice. I opened his door and saw that he was sitting upright on his bed and drawing in the dark. Using the same monotone expression, he told me he was *drawing me*.

This kind of thing makes me laugh. It's nothing outlandish or extreme. It's the beauty of the everyday moments of parenting. I kissed Madsen on the head and walked out of his room, his older brother passed out in the bed next to him. Before I had left his room, Madsen calmly instructed me to leave his door cracked. Of course.

Being a great parent is about showing love and strength through sacrifice. This isn't easy to do. I wake up every day fully realizing how much I fall short of my goal daily. How much I lack patience. How easy it is for me to focus on my own needs. Yet I wake up each morning and try again.

After all, watching the joy they have for life moves me. Watching the excitement they show with new experiences or new ideas. Getting the hug-assault when I come home from work each day. Meeting their needs and allowing our kids to thrive. The love a parent receives from a child fills us up in a special way. It is loving a rattlesnake that will bite you and then love you back.

If you've ever paid attention to the safety speech on an airplane (we all do, right?), you've no doubt heard them discuss the oxygen masks. You know, they'll fall from the ceiling but won't necessarily inflate, etc. The interesting thing to me has always been the very last part of the oxygen mask speech. That's where they instruct you to put on your mask first before helping those around you. The logic is simple: you aren't much help to others when you are passed out on the floor. It's always been a bizarre image for me to try and imagine one of my children sitting next to me in this scenario: face red without oxygen, eyes bulging in fear, little hand squeezing my arm, and me calmly explaining, "Hold on just a second, Daddy's mask isn't quite tight enough yet."

This has become a sort of running joke with Michelle and

me. She's never been great with setting up personal boundaries for herself. She's a type A person with an unbelievable drive for life and for the amount of things she thinks she can accomplish each day. As a result, this causes her to experience burnout moments of exhaustion. As her husband, there are times when I need to lovingly coach her (or when that doesn't work, strategically convince) to slow it down a bit to take care of herself.

If we go out of town together, I usually have to help her set a bedtime—literally a cutoff point—the night before when she will shut down the preparations and go to sleep. As we all know, there's always more to do.

My selfishness allows me to navigate the oxygen mask easier than my wife. I'll pack my bag first and then ask her what I can help with around the house. By that point she's already done a lot of it and we usually get into what we affectionately call the "oxygen mask conversation." I'll defend my actions by explaining I've first put my mask on so that now I can help.

At least one of us was listening on the plane.

I think we both tend to err on the opposite extremes. I can be so focused on what I personally need to get done (my oxygen mask) that I neglect to appropriately value the needs of my wife and kids (their oxygen masks). My wife can be so focused on the needs of our family (their oxygen masks) that she neglects to have anything left herself (to put on her mask). While it can be humorous at times, this dilemma presents a very real challenge for the way we live.

This is what parenting produces. It is a challenge unlike anything else we face but one that produces a unique pleasure unlike anything else.

INTENDED FOR GOOD

I've been a baseball fan since I was a little kid. Growing up in Arizona meant I didn't have a home team to root for since the Arizona Diamondbacks didn't exist until I was in junior high. That meant I had a sea of options to choose from when it came to finding a team to root for. As I mentioned in chapter 3, today I'm a huge New York Yankees fan. But it didn't start that way.

Growing up as a preacher's kid, we always had people around us. Over the years that meant I was influenced by different baseball fans in my life that determined which team I was rooting for. I started with the Minnesota Twins and later shifted to the Los Angeles Dodgers. I finally found reason and became a Yankees fan. But my era as a Dodgers fan set the stage for one of my favorite stories.

As a kid I didn't just like the team, I also liked a player in particular. Kids have an innate need for heroes. On the Twins it was Kirby Puckett. On the Yankees it was Don Mattingly. And on the Dodgers it was the great pitcher Orel Hershiser. I loved watching him on TV and collecting his baseball cards. Even better was the chance I had to see him pitch in a minor league game when he was rehabbing from an injury at one point in his career.

Orel Hershiser *was* the Dodgers to me.

One day I went to my dad's office after school, and he looked so excited that I knew something great was in store. With one hand behind his back, he told me he had a gift he wanted to give me. I could barely contain my excitement. When you're a kid, your parents have the ability to change your entire world in the blink of an eye.

That's when he handed me a baseball signed by Orel Hershiser.

I flipped out. I ran circles around his office, the hallway . . . everywhere. I held the ball in my hands like I was holding the Holy Grail itself. Here was a treasure signed by my hero! At some point during my lavish celebration, I noticed a weird look on my dad's face. He didn't look as happy as you'd expect given the excitement his gift just created in me. I paused for a moment to ask him what was wrong. Then he said four words that would forever change my life.

"I signed that ball."

I was stunned. I was embarrassed. I was angry. A swirl of emotions clouded my thoughts as I tried to make sense out of this revelation.

My dad looked profoundly sorry. He apologized over and over as he explained he thought this would just be a funny joke. He had no idea how excited I'd get by this ball. As anyone with kids knows, this is the story of parenting.

For those who know me, this might help explain why I'm a little off today.

Fast forward about two decades later. I told this story in a sermon at our church. It's fun to tell and instantly garners support from others when they hear it. But something interesting happened that particular morning. In the congregation of our church that day was the guy who oversaw the TV broadcast for the Arizona Diamondbacks. He works in the baseball industry and interacts with other teams of broadcasters such as those with ESPN. If you've ever watched an ESPN broadcast you know they have a wide variety of experts they use in their shows.

Which coincidentally included a now-retired player named Orel Hershiser.

When the guy at our church heard my story, he decided he would try to right this wrong. It wasn't too long afterward when he crossed paths with Orel and told him the story of the fake ball my dad gave me. The fact that Orel Hershiser heard my story is enough for me. It brings me a tremendous joy and a smile to my face when I think about it even today.

Weeks later, the guy from church pulled me aside and asked me to walk to his car with him. He had something he wanted to give me. He handed me a baseball with the following words on it: "To Jeremy, this is the real deal, Orel Hershiser."

Can you believe that?

Instantly, I reverted back to that elementary kid and wanted to run laps around the parking lot in excitement. I finally had my Orel Hershiser baseball. That's when a hauntingly dark thought overtook me. Was this another joke?

I looked at my friend and asked him point-blank if he had signed this ball. I had recovered from the wound from my dad but didn't know if I had it in me to recover from round two as an adult. He laughed at the question and reassured me this was in fact signed by the real Orel Hershiser.

As I held the ball in my hands, I felt a wave of excitement and satisfaction roll over me. But there was one thing I needed to do first.

I needed to show this to my dad.

I tracked him down that day and without a word handed him the ball to inspect. A smile crept over his face, and his excitement joined mine. I recapped the story of how I got it, and we both celebrated this moment together. Not seeming to realize he had just been redeemed for a past transgression, he pushed his luck with the next statement out of his mouth.

"If you think about it, you really have me to thank for getting you this."

Some people just don't know when to stop.

He explained that had he never forged the signature there would be no story for me to use to get the real thing. With what I can only describe as the spirit of God guiding my speech, I had a quick reply ready for him. I quoted a verse from the Old Testament and finally gave it the fulfillment it was always intended to have. Referencing back to the story of Joseph and his brothers, I said, "You intended to harm me, but God intended it for good."[1]

All parts of this story have become a treasured memory for me and my dad. But it reminds me that parents hold a unique power over their kids. In many ways, a parent creates the environments and situations for their kids to experience pleasure. But it goes beyond that since the degree to which a parent does this well often determines the pleasure the parent gets in his or her role. I know my dad felt awful when he saw my reaction to his joke. And I know he was genuinely pleased to see this story turn around years later. All engaged parents have these kinds of examples.

That's why I have many stories like this. I was blessed with both a dad and a mom who loved me immensely and invested greatly into my life. They are the first reason why the topic of parenting is a joy for me to talk about. I have an incredible relationship with them today, which makes telling stories like this fun.

Parents leave their kids with stories. Mine are fun to tell and make others laugh, but that isn't true for many kids. That's because parenting is hard. It can be even harder finding pleasure in it when you don't have a good example as I have.

THE MODEL DAD

Other than God Himself, who is the model dad in the Bible? Who is the guy we study to unpack wisdom from his parenting style? With as much history and as many stories as we find in the Bible, this should be a tough list to narrow down to only a few examples. I remember launching into this topic when I became a dad myself and realized how much I needed to learn. If you know the Bible well, think of any names that come to mind.

I asked this question on social media to gauge the collective thought and arrived at six names that topped the list. The main answers I received were the father of the prodigal son, Joseph (Mary's husband), Noah, Moses, Job, and Abraham.

At first glance it may appear an impressive list. But if we consider the names more carefully, it quickly becomes less impressive. The prodigal son's dad isn't a real person. This was a character Jesus made up in a story He once told.[2] We know next to nothing about Joseph, Noah, and Moses as fathers. We know that Job prayed for his kids, but they all died. And Abraham banished his firstborn son into the wilderness and almost killed his second son. This isn't exactly an easy list to use in order to acquire fatherhood advice!

Despite what the novelist Dan Brown may have you believe, Jesus never married and never had any kids. We might think to disqualify Him from the parenting conversation as a result. But being fully God and fully human allows Him to teach us in all areas, including this one.

There's a story about Jesus where two different lives intersect together in a profound moment of fatherly love.[3] One day a man named Jairus came to Him on behalf of his twelve-year-old daughter who was dying. Every moment counted, and Jairus made a huge gamble to leave his daughter's side to see if he could get Jesus' help. Amazingly, Jesus agreed, and they set off together to Jairus's home. I can imagine Jairus wanting to sprint home and eagerly counting the steps till they would arrive. Then the unthinkable happened: Jesus got distracted.

An adult woman approached Jesus while they were on their way. She had been bleeding for twelve years and no one could heal her. (The twelve years is significant because it's the same age as Jairus's daughter.) As Jesus walked through the crowd, she touched his cloak in hopes it would heal her, and shockingly, it did! But then Jesus stopped and asked the crowd who touched Him. I bet Jairus was hysterical on the inside at this point. His daughter was at home dying and here Jesus was stopping to talk with a sea of people.

After some confusion, the woman finally acknowledged she was the one who touched His cloak and experienced healing from it. This would have been a nerve-wracking moment as she had just committed a major taboo. She, an unclean woman, had touched a prophet. She had violated Old Testament law. Even worse, by Jewish standards she had just made Jesus unclean as well! She must have anticipated the coming wrath of Jesus and the crowd when they realized what she'd done. How sad to be healed by Jesus only to be killed by the crowd.

Instead, Jesus looked at her and said, "Daughter, your faith has healed you. Go in peace." It's amazing to note there is not even a hint of a reprimand. Jesus didn't worry about His own contamination or reputation. But the most profound part of His reply is easiest to miss. He called this woman "daughter." We might not realize how significant that detail is until we consider that this is the only woman in Scripture He ever called daughter. It wasn't a title He normally used. So why use it now?

Because Jairus was watching. Jairus stood there in agony as he waited for Jesus to attend to his own daughter. In an incredible display of love, Jesus put Himself into Jairus's shoes. And here we see that the sacrifice of a parent creates pleasure.

This is not your typical pleasure. This pleasure is deep and profound and often takes years to fully understand. This pleasure creates a bond unlike that of any other human relationship. This pleasure can instill worth and value in a person's soul. Jesus readily gave that to this suffering woman. He accepted her and allowed her to be accepted back into her culture.

But what about Jairus? While the story ends well for the adult woman, the story takes a heartbreaking turn for Jairus. It's at this point someone came to him with the news that his daughter had died. They didn't need to continue their journey. The gamble failed. He made the wrong decision and would likely spend the rest of his life regretting it.

Consider what Jairus must have felt. He had left his little girl's side in her final moments. He wasn't there. And he couldn't save her. That is a grief unlike any other. Ask any parent who has had to bury a child. But Jesus simply told him to believe and not let his fear overwhelm him. He continued the walk to Jairus's home. When Jesus arrived, He informed the mourners to stop crying. He then took the little girl by the hand and revived her. He said to her, "My child, get up!" Here was Jesus speaking fatherly love in sacrifice. Again ignoring the social taboos, He touched a dead body and brought this child back to life. If Jesus wasn't already unclean from the bleeding woman, touching this dead body would have sealed the deal.

In great biblical understatement, we read that "her parents were astonished." That's the pleasure of parenting done right. In both of these examples, people asked Jesus for healing, and He gave that plus compassion. That's where parenting starts, with meeting needs. But pleasure in parenting doesn't end there. The sacrifice of a parent can also create pleasure.

In Jesus, we see the love of a parent modeled for us to emulate, and we also experience the love of the parent we need as well. That's the interesting part about parenting. If you have no kids of your own, or if you have a couple of kids, or even a lot of kids, you still had parents of your own. I suppose this logic will become more complicated as science continues to make it easier for us to reproduce in nontraditional ways, but for now this applies to most people. In parenting, we pursue pleasure through investing in ourselves in a profound way in the lives of others. And in parenting we pursue God, through meeting our own needs and participating in the process of new life all around us.

Parenting invites a person to participate in life and in God in profound ways. And there is pleasure there.

RAISING A BORROWED SNAKE

In my own parenting I've also had the chance to be a foster dad. This is the bizarre experience of raising someone else's child as your own. You live on borrowed time with no guarantee of tomorrow. Parenting means giving of yourself for someone, and foster parenting adds the dimension of giving of yourself for someone most people don't want. It aligns your heart with the overlooked and oppressed in ways that are nearly impossible to do on your own.

Earlier this chapter I explained my two expectations for future parents: (1) it will be harder than anything you've ever done, but (2) it will be more fulfilling than anything you've done. Parenting a foster child puts both of these on steroids. The challenges of normal parenting are still there, but you now add the state system, unnatural emotional boundaries, estranged family members, and complete lack of control of the situation, to name just a few issues.

But in raising a foster child you have the opportunity to change someone's story forever, which is an opportunity that is hard to compare to anything else. My three biological kids were each born into a certain trajectory in life. Our foster child was born into a completely different story, which we have been working to change. The other day someone looked at our littlest one (whom we've fostered) and made the comment that he is so lucky. They obviously said this as a compliment to Michelle and me and the life we can offer him that is different from what he had been born into.

> **Parenting, especially through fostering and adoption, allows you to experience the very heartbeat of God.**

But I responded by saying I believe the opposite is true. He is incredibly unlucky. Why was he born into a set of challenges that I will truly never experience? Why was the deck stacked against him from day one?

We got our foster child when he was three weeks old. We had no idea what to expect. He weighed only five pounds and was smaller than my daughter Adelyn's baby doll. The strangest thing we noticed in those early days was that he never cried. I mean ever. When we'd put him down to sleep at night, we had to set an alarm for when we would wake him up to eat. At his size we had to be diligent early on to help him grow. We'd go to get him out of his crib, assuming he was asleep, only to find him quietly lying awake. He was hungry, but he'd learned that there was no point in crying to try and get his needs met.

While at first thought, a baby who doesn't cry may sound like a great problem to have, it was one of the most heartbreaking realities of what we were doing. Healthy babies cry. And healthy babies do a lot of things that parents tend to take for granted.

In parenting our foster child, we experience the pleasure of his changed story and the pleasure of getting to participate in something holy and supernatural. The brother of Jesus once wrote that "religion that God our Father accepts as pure and faultless is this: to look after orphans and widows in their distress and to keep oneself from being polluted by the world."[4]

Parenting, especially through fostering and adoption, allows you to experience the very heartbeat of God. When you connect with God in this way, you cannot help but feel the pleasure from it. As David Platt has argued, "We care for orphans not because we are rescuers, but because we are the rescued." We extend this pleasure to others when we experience it ourselves. This goes back to what we saw with Jesus in the role of a parent.

A surprising pleasure has been the effect fostering has had on our other kids. Not only has it made us better parents, but it has also brought out something in them I could have never produced otherwise. I remember our classes we had to take to become licensed foster parents and the training we underwent to learn what to look for in kids who have certain developmental challenges. One day they talked about something called sensory processing disorder (a concept and term I didn't know existed) and some of the signs of it. The point was that this was common in foster kids. But as we listened to some of the details they shared, Michelle and I both looked at each other in amazement. That's because one of our three biological children did all those things too!

We had concluded it was either a personality trait or a sign of disobedience, but that day we realized it was something totally different. After getting our child tested and confirming that this was indeed the case, we have been able to parent so much more effectively. We've literally seen a different kid emerge since we've known what to look for and how to respond better. That was a huge unintended blessing.

Another surprising pleasure for our family has been watching the way our kids treat their foster sibling. While they understand something is different about his story, they don't treat him differently. They adore him. They care for him, cuddle with him, and sometimes take things from him like they do with each other. But having him around has also created a tender heart for others in my kids. Our kids will now ask us questions about other kids they meet or hear about in need of help.

When our oldest son, Gavin, had a kid in his class at school labeled as a "bully," we ended up being called in about it because Gavin was the only kid who was always around him. The teachers knew Gavin didn't have a history of misbehaving but thought that his friendship with this other kid was strange. When I asked him about it, Gavin told me that he was trying to help this kid because he didn't have any friends and didn't know how he should act. Gavin was in kindergarten.

And this is the beautiful part of parenting so many people miss out on or never seem to embrace. No matter how many kids you have or whether you foster or adopt, whenever you pour yourself out for others, you experience a profound pleasure in the process. You end up meeting a deep need in yourself and connecting with God in ways you cannot even articulate. And you can do this whether the kids are biologically yours, whether they live with you, whether you are a grandparent, an aunt or uncle, or whether you are just a trusted voice of influence in their life. It's not about how many kids you can afford, or have time for, or whether you or not you are a "kid person."

I recently read an amazing post from a mother of five kids about how many kids you should have. She was about to adopt number six, after already having five at home. In a great play of irony, she explained that having more kids wasn't to meet a need, but that there's a greater pleasure in it.

> What I want is to get to the end of my wants. I want to get to the end of controlling and taking on only what I can do. I want the immense privilege of seeing what God can do through me. That fills me with unspeakable, illogical joy at the prospect of being used as He wills. I have a Christ-like love for a child who is not my own and all the anticipation of Christmas at the gift—the privilege—of being his mother, no matter the cost.[5]

Unspeakable, illogical joy is a great way of describing parenting.

CHAPTER EIGHT

GLITZ, GLAM, AND GOD

"If we value the pursuit of knowledge, we must be free
to follow wherever that search may lead us."

Adlai Stevenson

IT CAN BE STRESSFUL having a social life around certain Christians. Many of them have strict limits about R-rated movies and secular music in addition to a score of rules about all sorts of other media. It can easily cause them to live sheltered lives with a false sense of the real world.

But is the alternative to have no filter? To consume anything and everything in our pursuit of entertainment? As anyone who has been swayed negatively by entertainment knows, it isn't always beneficial. While the specifics aren't spelled out for us in the Bible with today's media, Scripture can still help us navigate our way through Hollywood.

But applying faith to forms of entertainment gets tricky. Should Christians watch R-rated movies? And if we are comfortable saying yes to this, which types of R-rated movies are okay? As a kid who grew up in a Christian environment, I quickly learned that certain forms of entertainment are worse than others. For example, a typical Christian might be fine with an R-rated movie if it includes graphic violence but not if it includes nudity or sexuality.

I've always found this a little silly.

True, some people have a sensitivity to portrayals of sexual encounters that affects them differently than watching violence. But the reverse is also true. And this has nothing to do with one of them being more spiritually acceptable than the other. Sadly, in lieu of any formal criteria to use in entertainment, we follow the majority.

We have a general tendency to think that the more people believe something, the more it must be true or valuable. This is faulty thinking for a number of reasons. Reality is reality regardless of how many people believe it. It matters not today that the majority opinion used to be the earth was flat. We know that's not reality. This applies to a myriad of examples like alchemy, the four humors, spontaneous generation, celestial immutability, emission theory (not what you might assume it is), or bloodletting. The fact you likely aren't familiar with all—or any—of these practices is my point. These were once popular beliefs that are no longer popular.

Ideas, like teenage pop stars, struggle to maintain popularity through the years. That's why it's important to approach ideas with an equal skepticism regardless of their acceptance at the time. What's popular today may not be popular tomorrow. More importantly, what's in favor today may not actually be valuable. This doesn't make less popular beliefs somehow more true. The point is that popularity is a bad gauge for verifying truth.

We also need to consider that if all we know is what's popular, we are missing out on a lot of other ideas. As the marketing guru Seth Godin wrote on his blog,

When you only listen to the top 40, you're letting the crowd decide what you hear. And if you consume nothing but the most liked, the most upvoted, the most viral, the most popular, you've abdicated responsibility for your incoming. Most people only read bestselling books. That's what makes them bestsellers, after all . . . Popular is not the same as important, or often, not the same as good.[1]

When it comes to our search for pleasure in entertainment, we can't follow the crowd. This presents a problem, because the crowd controls the entertainment we experience. The crowd owns entertainment. And it's nearly impossible for you to see reality clearly in the midst of the crowd.

In 1951, a guy named Solomon Asch designed an experiment to test just how far a crowd could distort a person's view of reality. In the experiment, only one of the participants is legitimately a participant. The other seven people around him are secretly in on it. The researchers asked the group to look at images of three lines next to each other of differing lengths and determine which one was the longest. This wasn't a subjective question, nor was it difficult to figure out the correct answer. You wouldn't think there is any way to get a discrepancy of answers. But after the first couple of rounds went as planned, the other participants began to answer the question wrong. They intentionally choose the wrong line, yet they each agreed with each other. Shockingly, the only participant

> The crowd controls the entertainment we experience. The crowd owns entertainment. And it's nearly impossible for you to see reality clearly in the midst of the crowd.

truly being measured began to go along with the group and chose the wrong answer even though he didn't agree with what he was choosing. In fact, if you watch some of the videos of the experiment, you can visibly see the tension on the person's face as he answers the questions.

Asch found that three out of four people intentionally chose the wrong answer to conform to the crowd on at least one question. That means only a fourth of the people were able to resist this urge to fit in![2] Nobody wants to be the odd man out.

I remember experiencing this my first year in junior high. I was a small kid, but I didn't realize how small I was until we had to record our body weight one day in our PE class. All the boys lined up in the locker room. Each boy stood on a scale as our coach said our weight and another coach recorded it. Standing in the back part of the line, I remember listening to each of the numbers before me. All of them were above one hundred pounds, some of them by quite a bit. Then it got to me, and I was the first boy to be under a hundred pounds. I don't necessarily remember getting picked on for that moment. But I vividly remember how out of place I felt. Strange how those memories stick with us decades later. I bet you have your own stories from childhood that prove the same point. That time you struggled to control your bladder, or said something stupid, or did something everyone else laughed at. We learn early on not to offend the crowd or the emotional damage will be severe. The crowd punishes those who disagree with it or behave different from it.

So what happens if the crowd tells us the most pleasurable forms of entertainment but we suspect it might be wrong? According to social psychology, we'd still go along with it at the expense of actual pleasure! Regardless of your personal stance on God, I bet you still have had a sense that there's something missing, something empty, about the way we go after pleasure in our culture. Most people push back a nagging sense that they seem to be stuck in a losing game no one is willing to stop playing.

Mark Twain once cautioned, "Whenever you find yourself on the side of the majority, it is time to pause and reflect." This is the conundrum, because we want to be on the side of the majority, especially when it comes to having a good time. Would you rather have less pleasure with the crowd, or more pleasure outside of the crowd?

Think about the clothes you wear. Think about your hairstyle, the way you talk, the vehicle you drive, or the music you listen to. Think about the ways you spend a Friday night or what you choose to do when you hang out with your friends. Do you become a different person depending on who you are around?

I see this happen often whenever I meet someone new, especially when I'm traveling. We'll often be midway into a conversation when they ask me what I do for a living. As with my banking friend from earlier, my answer tends to produce a funny reaction in people as they replay all the things they've just said to me. Their language has a weird way of sounding different once they know I'm a pastor.

Unless you plan to join a monastery, you're going to have to navigate the crowd. So how do we know which line is actually the longest line and which is the right answer? What pursuits of entertainment are actually the most pleasurable? We may not always confidently know the answer, but we can confidently know that the crowd is not a trustworthy source for it. Instead of following the crowd, we must go back to the Designer and find something we can measure our entertainment against. Because this is so difficult to do in the midst of the crowd, I've found two simple questions to be extremely helpful.

WHAT IS TRUE?

I've always appreciated a biblical guy named Daniel. He can be found in an Old Testament book with his name. Daniel was an Israelite but found himself living in another nation under a foreign power. I find this to be incredibly insightful as America completes the transition out of Christendom (where Christians are the majority and have the power). Daniel also had a few friends who together modeled faithfulness to God in the midst of some challenging circumstances. One verse in particular stands out to me. In describing Daniel and his friends, the Bible says, "To these four young men God gave knowledge and understanding of all kinds of literature and learning. And Daniel could understand visions and dreams of all kinds."[3]

I love that God gives them something we don't normally attribute to God: literature, learning, and the understanding of visions and dreams. This knowledge goes far beyond an understanding of the Hebrew Scriptures. A modern-day parallel might read like this: "To these four young men God gave understanding of Dostoyevsky, Dickens, and Shakespeare. He also gave knowledge of string theory, quantum physics, and relativity. And Daniel could understand visions and dreams better than Sigmund Freud."

Wouldn't that be awesome?

We normally exclude God from these types of conversations rather than look to Him for insight into them. Many conservative forms of Christianity even forbid them. If we exclude God from any conversation, we do so to our own detriment. Christians are comfortable thinking of Jesus as an expert in spiritual things, but we might not look to Him to help us with our car repairs. Yet this dichotomy shows a limitation of our sense of compartmentalization, not of God. We saw this in the last chapter in the role of Jesus as a father (even though He had no biological kids of His own).

A biblical understanding of truth comes from realizing all truth belongs to God. Which means truth can be found in just about anything. This means even "secular" areas! I hope this is painfully obvious, but I fear it needs to be stated.

This gives us the first criteria through which to navigate entertainment for a greater pleasure. As we look at all sorts of entertainment, we must ask ourselves, "What is true?" The apostle Paul said it like this: "Finally, brothers and sisters, whatever is true, whatever is noble, whatever is right, whatever is pure, whatever is lovely, whatever is admirable—if anything is excellent or praiseworthy—think about such things."[4]

Contrast this to the normal questions we ask about entertainment.

What is popular?

What is funny?

What is available?

What do my friends like?

Instead, we should ask what is true.

And finding truth in entertainment doesn't just mean we find things we can trace back to a Bible verse. Truth can be a depiction of pain, or loss, or sadness, or any number of aspects of what it means to be human (and these are all in the pages of Scripture as well). In fact, secular entertainment captures much of what is true about the human experience in ways the church rarely feels comfortable doing.

I'm grateful for the insights of guys like Brett McCracken. Brett serves as the editor for Biola University's *Biola Magazine*. In that role he finds himself watching a lot of movies, especially movies the majority Christian crowd might not attend. In thinking about making art as a Christian, Brett offered the following advice in *Hipster Christianity*:

> We should simply focus on our craft, on making the best art we can. We should understand that people will and should resonate with our work not because it is Christian but because it is good. Above all, Christians should make good art, true art; art unafraid of exploring mystery, portraying evil, and looking for truth wherever it appears. Which is exactly what the best secular artists are doing.

Like finding treasure buried underground, we sometimes search through dirt in order to find a gem of truth. How much we search through, and which areas we search, depends on the second question we should ask.

WHAT IS BENEFICIAL?

What should you do when you enjoy a pleasure but someone else around you struggles with it? Music is a great example. Music can sway the emotions of my wife both positively and negatively. I'm more of an immovable object with the music I'm listening to.

The best example I have of this comes from a conversation

with my dad when I was in junior high. Like many parents of adolescents, he didn't approve of my musical selection. The conversation erupted when I brought home a new Metallica album one night. When we both made our arguments, we realized we were at an impasse. That's when we made a deal. If he could prove that listening to Metallica negatively affected my behavior, then I would surrender my CDs. Until then, he would let me listen to what I wanted. We both walked away thinking we'd worked the other person over. This is common for men.

But I never had to surrender my Metallica CDs. And he eventually believed that for me, they didn't have a negative impact. But that isn't true for everyone.

The greatest part of this story is that years later, my dad and I were able to spend an evening with James Hetfield (the lead singer of Metallica) and tell him our story. Not only is Hetfield a surprisingly nice guy in person, he also seemed quite entertained by our battle all those years ago.[5]

Since my wife and I respond to music differently, I let Michelle pick the music in the car. It's usually something I find too upbeat or cheesy, but it puts her in a good frame of mind. The balance is that my music doesn't negatively affect her (because she's not listening to it) and I don't have to listen to her music when she's not in the car.

That's the spirit of what Paul taught in the book of Romans we looked at in our discussion on alcohol. Elsewhere in chapter 14 Paul wrote,

Therefore let us stop passing judgment on one another. Instead, make up your mind not to put any stumbling block or obstacle in the way of a brother or sister. I am convinced, being fully persuaded in the Lord Jesus, that nothing is unclean in itself. But if anyone regards something as unclean, then for that person it is unclean.[6]

If we apply Paul's logic to the way we interact with entertainment, we have another principle with which to navigate. As relativistic as it sounds, some entertainment might be beneficial for me and not for you. And what is fine for you might not be beneficial for me. Whereas the first question of what is true should be ultimately agreed upon, the second question of what is beneficial must be contextualized for each of us.

> Unlike the first question (what is true?), the second question (what is beneficial?) demands a certain level of subjectivity that requires a person of maturity to apply.

As we see in other areas like sexuality, what brings each person pleasure can vary. When it comes to entertainment, that can be the case as well, often dramatically. Instead of looking to the crowd, we must spend the time to determine for ourselves whether the things our friends enjoy have the same effect on us. They may be true, but are they beneficial? Not just beneficial to those around you, but beneficial to you? This is the part most people miss. We automatically assume if it's beneficial for someone, it must automatically be beneficial for me. But that is often not the case.

I don't watch scary movies. I *want* to watch scary movies, and I *used* to watch scary movies, but I don't watch scary movies anymore. That's because scary movies mess me up. At the risk of sounding lame, the movie that became the turning point for me was the 2002 film called *The Ring*. I loved the movie, but I couldn't turn off the weird thoughts it gave me for approximately seven days afterward (that joke makes sense if you've seen the movie). I still get invited to watch scary movies. And I've had to get used to declining these invitations in my pursuit of pleasure in entertainment.

Think about your own enjoyment of entertainment. Can you think of any areas that are not as beneficial for you as they are for your friends? Do you feel comfortable telling your friends this or opting out? If not, you are stuck in the Asch experiment and missing out on a bigger pleasure.

Christians have a tendency to take this concept and apply our own criteria on behalf of God for others. It's easy for me to expect that everyone around me should avoid watching scary movies as well. But I have to remember that scary movies don't affect everyone the way they affect me. That's the point Paul made. Unlike the first question (what is true?), the second question (what is beneficial?) demands a certain level of subjectivity that requires a person of maturity to apply. If there is truth in it, entertainment can be a way for a person to experience both pleasure and God even if it isn't beneficial to me.

Think about the areas of entertainment you personally have a sensitivity to more than others. You may have created boundaries for yourself and your family as a result. It might mean you don't watch R-rated movies or listen to secular music. Now consider the tougher question: Do you expect those around you to respond like you do in this area? Most of us do this without even realizing it. This will put you on the fast track to becoming the type of person known for robbing an experience of pleasure for those around you.

Instead, learn your own limits of what is beneficial and allow those around you to create their own.

KIDS AND BABY MEN

It's not just movies and music anymore. Today's technology allows for new forms of entertainment that were impossible for previous generations. Consider just one of these fairly new examples in video games.

I've only understood the novelty of video games in recent years. I always thought it was a bit strange my dad could never help me beat a level in Mario, but it wasn't until I started helping my own kids with their video games that the contrast became fully evident. I had the privilege of growing up at the same time Nintendo began to take over the world. While that was awesome for my childhood, it left me with a distorted reality of the impact of video games. My dad's favorite video game from his childhood involved a handheld football game with little red dots that moved across the field. Now my kids are growing up with a sophistication of games unthinkable even in my childhood.

I realize most people who read this probably do not play video games themselves. In fact, I hesitate to talk about how much I enjoy playing video games for the simple reason that I know it is one of the most misunderstood and abused forms of entertainment out there.

To those on the outside, video games are often assumed to be for one of two people: (1) kids; or (2) adult men who can't grow up and don't have boundaries or discipline. It is true these two groups represent much of video game consumers, if not most. But they do not represent all. I personally enjoy playing Xbox games, and I have a healthy marriage, four amazing kids, and a career I'm proud of. To me, a good video game is like reading a good fictional novel and provides a way for my mind to relax and for my imagination muscles to be flexed. Like most things in life, video games should be enjoyed with boundaries, and when they are not, or when a person cannot maintain control, it is probably best to avoid them. My wife and I don't get into fights over me playing video games (which is not true for most guys from what I hear).

One of the themes I've noticed with video games is that they highlight the more fun parts of life and omit the tedious parts (choosing keyframes over inbetweens). Because of this, it is a relaxing way to enjoy a story. Before you write this off as totally unhealthy, consider that TV, movies, and books do the same thing. How much of a TV show is spent depicting the characters eating, sleeping, or stopping to use the restroom? Those are very real parts of life, yet they get very little coverage in our entertainment. I remember watching the show *24* and noticing Jack Bauer never needed to eat or use the restroom for twenty-four hours straight!

My friend Paul and I both like to play video games, and neither of us fit the gamer stereotype. Paul is about ten years older than I am and has a family and a career as well. In fact, Paul is so weird he gets up crazy early in the morning to play.

I love to talk with Paul about video-game morality. We stumbled into this conversation as we were discussing a game we had both played. It was one of those single-player games where you are a character in a story and you follow that person's life throughout the game. One day our nonchalant conversation developed a deeper tone.

"Did you get married in the game?" Paul asked me.

"Of course," I said. "Didn't you?"

"No way. I already have a wife."

Cue the confusion at this point. I'm perplexed at how having a wife in real life negated his video-game character getting married in the game. And we're not talking about getting married to another real person using a different video game character, but rather a scripted computer character built into the game and into the main storyline.

"Does Michelle know you got married in the game?" Paul asked me.

"Yeah, she was sitting on the couch next to me when I did it."

Paul looked stunned. I couldn't tell whether he was more bothered by me or by my wife. "Don't you think it's weird you would get married in the game if you already have a wife?"

Aware we approached this discussion from dramatically different angles, I responded by telling him that I am not my character. I'm playing through a fictional character in a fictional story (all of which has been computerized). Paul didn't seem impressed by my answer. So I decided to contextualize it for him.

"Did you kill people in the game?" I asked him.

"Of course," he replied.

"Would you kill people in real life?"

He gave me an absurd look and muttered something about that not being real. At this point, we could finally agree. But this conversation illustrated for me the growing tensions of morality in an ever-evolving entertainment arena.

While it's easy for me to separate a game I'm playing from my real life, it might not be so easy in the years to come. I'm sure pornography will continue to adapt and include more interactive involvement through video-game technology. The lines will continually be blurred.

While not as popular as it once was, platforms like Second Life allow users to have a digital version of themselves interact online with digital versions of other real life people. The game advertises itself as "the largest-ever 3D virtual world created entirely by its users."[7] Getting married in Second Life (to a digital version of a real person) is very different from getting married to a computerized storyline. But how do we navigate this? And what do we do when this gets harder to distinguish between in our real and virtual worlds?

What we find is the subjectivity of morality in entertainment. Instead of navigating this through what feels right to us or what the crowd decides (which leads to a hazy approach of pleasure), we instead should ask about what is true and what is beneficial. I submit that while these questions don't solve the tension, asking them helps us tackle each new specific area of entertainment we seek to enjoy.

CHAPTER NINE

COMPETITION VS. COMMUNITY

"When we open ourselves up to love, we do not leave pain behind in favor of pleasure; rather we open ourselves up to an experience of depth and meaning that involves both pain and pleasure. For when life is infused with depth and wonder, we cannot help but experience our fair share of both happiness and unhappiness. It is only in protecting ourselves from love that we can hope to protect ourselves from suffering."

Peter Rollins

WE'VE SEEN IN THE LAST FEW CHAPTERS many of the specifics we often focus on for pleasure. But just as we counterintuitively learn that pleasure flows best from the limits of design, so also we find that pleasure results from often unexpected places. And often in unexpected ways. And it turns out it's all around you.

Specifically, *they* are all around you.

We essentially classify the crowd around us as either competition or community (my alliteration is acting up again). It feels natural to view others as competition to beat, to one-up, to inch out. Or we can instead focus on the people around us and build them into a new type of community. Treating people simply along these lines alone will set you apart from the crowd. But more than that, we choose to put others before ourselves.

As you might imagine, I'm going to propose that this is actually a powerful way to find pleasure and a tangible way to follow God. We live in a world that tells us to take care of ourselves. And it isn't like we need much encouragement in that area. It's what we naturally think to do! That's why the thought of treating those around us with a priority over ourselves is such a radical thought. Here again we explore a concept deep in delayed gratification, as we've already seen. I sacrifice—maybe even suffer—now for the sake of someone else. Sound awful?

My friend Tim does an amazing job with this. He's a huge extrovert. Anyone who comes within a few feet in proximity of him ends up in a conversation. He's a fellow New York Yankees fan, and I got the chance to experience a game with him in New York. In the middle of the game, a foul ball flew at a fan in a section close to ours. After the initial confusion, he emerged victorious with the ball in his hand. If you've ever been to a baseball game, this is a common occurrence. But then something uncommon happened.

My friend Tim stood up and yelled at this guy to get his attention. "Hey!"

The introvert in me began to go into my shell. Tim was attracting attention to himself, and I was sitting next to him. But Tim didn't stop after one shout. He kept yelling. Finally it turned into something like, "Hey, guy with the foul ball!"

Finally, he turned toward us. That's when Tim shouted something awful.

"You should give my friend the ball."

At this point, all the fans in the seats locked in on this very audible conversation happening between sections. And I slowly started to sink down in my seat to avoid their stares.

"Why?" shouted the fan in return. I thought he had a good point.

"Because he's from Arizona. He's never seen baseball!"

I should point out that Tim is also a pastor. But baseball makes people do weird things. After a moment of consideration and a long, uncomfortable stare at me, the fan yelled back, "But he's wearing a Yankees jersey!" Again, this was another solid point. Not only was I wearing my favorite Jeter jersey, I was also wearing one of many Yankee hats I own.

"I just bought that for him!" Tim replied.

Tim didn't get me the ball that day, but I got to see a hilarious portrayal of how to choose community over competition up close.

Something profound happens when we treat others like this, when we start living through community. We begin to experience love in dramatic new ways. And I'm not talking about giving out hugs to everyone you see. In fact, looking at others as community often involves behaviors we tend to assume shouldn't belong.

TALK IT OUT

It may come as a surprise that a discussion on valuing others above ourselves involves difficult conversations. Sadly, *conflict* is a word most people associate with unhealthy relationships. Without realizing it, we tend to lump conflict into the list of negative behaviors to avoid.

I've found that everyone naturally lands somewhere on a

conflict scale. Many people are conflict averse and hate the idea of talking through an issue or addressing it head-on. In fact, this is most people. If that's you, consider speaking up when you feel something strongly with a friend, despite a fear of where the conversation might go.

Other people have a natural tolerance for the awkward moments of conflict. If that's you, you may need to consider keeping some of your opinions to yourself. There's a fine line between being truthful and being a jerk! This is definitely the side I'm on, and I've had to learn that I can't always tackle every issue I have an opinion about.

My point here is not to show one as good and one as bad. You are what you are when it comes to your wiring for conflict. My mom tends to avoid conflict and my dad tends to quickly embrace it. This has allowed me to see the differences firsthand and to also see how they blend or oppose each other (the conflict styles, not my parents). In my own marriage, both Michelle and I are comfortable with conflict. This creates a unique dynamic in our household.

Michelle and I share a belief that there are no issues in our marriage we can't solve as long as we have a willingness to talk about it and work on it. This means we talk about everything. And because of our conflict styles, these tend to be energetic discussions. We created argument boundaries early on so we argue without raising our voices or calling each other names. But within our safe conflict environment, we don't pretend or hope the other person gets our point. We make sure they do.

For conflict-averse readers, this might sound terrifying. We'll often hear people tell us they enjoy spending time with us since they get to "overhear" our conversations as they happen. Evidently others are either surprised or at least entertained by the way we work through differing opinions. The point is that if you hang out with us often enough, you'll see just how many of these conversations take place.

I've found a willingness to have tough conversations produces a greater pleasure as a result. Our marriage is far healthier because we deal with issues as they come up. In the workplace, the same concept applies. Would you want to work at a place where you never quite know where you stand and you never quite know how to get better? What an awful feeling to show up to work wondering whether you are about to get promoted or about to get fired.

Honesty—communicated in love—is a tremendous gift you give to others. Honesty communicated without love is a poor example of conflict. But that shouldn't keep us from learning the healthy expression of it. According to Douglas Stone and Sheila Heen, authors of *Thanks for the Feedback*, we must consider the different categories of feedback we receive from others.

> The very first task in assessing feedback is figuring out what kind of feedback we are dealing with. Broadly, feedback comes in three forms: appreciation (thanks), coaching (here's a better way to do it), and evaluation (here's where you stand).

If we view conflict as negative, we'll struggle to communicate truthfully. As a result, we'll experience less pleasure overall in our relationships with those around us. While appreciation might be the area most people feel comfortable speaking to others, coaching and evaluation will definitely require a dose of conflict. Think of the most meaningful relationships in your life and the people who have caused you to grow. I'll bet they were willing to have a tough conversation with you at some point. I'll bet they gave you a sense of appreciation, but also provided coaching and evaluation along the way. Friends like that are a gift. They care more about your relationship than the momentary awkwardness of your reaction.

The end result is that we know where we stand with those around us and are free from second-guessing ourselves (evaluation), we continue to grow personally and discover we are different than we used to be (coaching), and we feel valued by those we respect and love (appreciation). That's a great example of pleasure. Do you have people in your life who will have that type of conversation with you? More importantly, are you willing to have that conversation with someone else?

BETTER THAN RECEIVING

We've each heard the expression, especially around Christmastime: "It's better to give than to receive." But does anyone truly believe this?

It sure seems doubtful, at least the majority of the time. But more importantly, this expression comes from the master pleasure-contrarian Himself: Jesus.[1] Jesus expertly challenged the ways in which people pursued pleasure, and here He taught an important concept.

It's hard for children, and even adults, to fully embrace this catchy little saying because receiving feels pretty awesome. "Gifts" is even one of the five love languages.[2] But as we see with love languages, what we tend to do for others is also what we want done for us. For those of us with one of the other four love languages, we must learn to heighten our sense of giving to others, not only for their pleasure, but for ours.

My wife, Michelle, and I wanted to celebrate our thirtieth birthdays with a big celebration. Our birthdays are four months apart so we decided to combine them for a memorable night. We saved for a long time in order to do something out of the ordinary. We ended up renting out the second-floor balcony of a restaurant and inviting thirty of our closest friends and family. Our goal was simple: to celebrate the thirty people in our lives who had impacted us by our thirtieth birthdays. Thirty for thirty.

As with wedding planning, this list was difficult to determine. There were many people who should have been there, but we simply couldn't invite them if we wanted to reach our target number. We needed a smaller group for what we had in mind. We even themed the night with bow ties (for men) and bows (for women). From the moment of the invite, it was obvious people didn't know what to expect. I was asked frequently whether the bow tie thing was serious. Did I really expect them to buy one just for this night? Absolutely.

When everyone showed up that evening, attired in bows and bow ties, we welcomed them to a night of memories. One guy showed up in a regular straight tie, which I promptly cut it into a bow tie with a knife. It didn't look as bad as you might think.

Because we had saved specifically for the occasion, we paid for the all the food and drinks. We even brought in a cigar roller who gave out stogies to anyone who wanted them. Neither my wife nor I thought much of this. It cost us a chunk of change, but we thought of it as money well spent. We had wanted to do this for a while, saved for it, and had a good reason to celebrate. What caught us by surprise was the confusion this caused. Many people didn't understand why we were the ones paying for everything.

On our birthdays we wanted to give a gift to those closest to us. I don't say that to brag on my wife and me or to try to impress you. Think of it in more selfish terms. We got to plan an evening with the people we wanted to be around doing the things we like to do. And we were able to provide them an evening of pleasant surprises in the process.

> Think about the last time you gave someone a gift that caused them to light up in excitement and joy … What would it take for you to do that more often with more people?

The joy Michelle and I received from watching our friends left a lasting impression on us.

I wish I could afford to give gifts to others like that every night. That's because giving offers a pleasure unlike the pleasure we receive from getting something. The challenge is giving takes work. To be in a position to give good gifts to others you have to either be extremely thoughtful or have margin to use; often both. That's why we don't do it more often.

But what if we planned our lives around allowing us to experience pleasures like this? Michelle and I decided years ago to save enough in our bank accounts to have margin for special giving as needs came up. We know there will always be opportunities for giving, but we will not always in a place to do something about it unless we plan accordingly. In the church, we often use words like *giving* and *stewardship* interchangeably. But they each show another side of the coin. Without stewardship (the way you manage your money, especially with the view that it belongs to God), giving can really only happen rarely. Regular giving requires a plan to ensure you have something available to give. But that also means you are saving up for future pleasure.

This may sound like a purely spiritual argument. But think about the last time you gave someone a gift that caused them to light up in excitement and joy. What was the occasion? What did it cost you, both financially and emotionally? How excited were you to give the gift and how did it feel when you saw their reaction to it? More importantly, what would it take for you to do that more often with more people?

With this memory fresh in your mind, consider Jesus' words again. Does your feeling of giving outmatch what you feel when you receive?

I think about guys like Alan and Eric Barnhart, who in 2007 gave away 99 percent of their company—worth hundreds of millions of dollars. It is telling to hear Alan talk about why they did something like that.

> The company has been able to give away tens of millions of dollars and is involved in all kinds of ministries. It has been a real treat. Some people would say that you're crazy to do that, that's nuts. But I don't think it's crazy at all. I think it's perfectly logical. I think it makes perfect sense.[3]

Sure, Alan would consider himself a Christian. That part is obvious when you hear him tell his story. But what I find fascinating is his reason for giving away 99 percent of his phenomenally successful company wasn't because "Jesus said so," or "the Bible said so." In that case we might detect a hint of bitterness or reluctance. Rather, Alan pointed to the fact it was "perfectly logical." To him, it made "perfect sense." He began with the logic of Jesus but didn't leave it there. He tested it himself. Alan and Eric have processed the words of Jesus and seen the logic behind them firsthand. As Anne Frank observed, "No one has ever become poor by giving."

Alan and Eric have seen through the deception of pleasure. There is no end to the incredibly moving stories we see from all sorts of people like this. You've no doubt experienced a taste of it yourself in your own life. How much more pleasure would we receive if we truly challenged ourselves to give more than we think possible?

THE MOST UNPOPULAR WORD EVER

It's easy to think of putting others first in all of the easy areas and doing things for the people we like. But how does choosing community over competition change the way we view everyone around us? How does it change the way we view those people who oppose us or actively work against us in one way or another? To see how this might apply, I invite you to think for a moment on your view of the word *surrender*.

It's usually the last resort for a person who has tried everything else. For a person who has been outmatched by another. For a person defeated. As such, we dread the thought of having to surrender.

But what if we actually chose surrender, even when we weren't forced to? If we gave up our need to ensure the ends no matter the means? What if we realized that in our need to ensure a forced victory we accepted an unnatural burden?

More than that, what if we actually found pleasure in surrender?

Since you likely don't have an army at your disposal while you wage a formal war on another nation, surrender means more than just our traditional definition. I've found in today's world our concept of surrender connects to our concept of violence, or nonviolence as it were. To examine nonviolence is to examine the essence of surrender, albeit from an outside perspective that allows us to see our value system. Here I want to touch on a challenging concept that tends to create more questions than it provides answers. But I've found that truth has a funny way of acting like that.

I grew up in Arizona. For those of you who may not know, Arizona is still the Wild, Wild West. Gun ownership, in fact concealed gun carry, is the norm for many people. Arizona might be second only to Texas in this regard. I was raised in a culture with a love for guns and the power they bring. I spent no time debating the thought of defending my family with a gun. It wasn't even an issue. Of course I would use a gun to protect my family, and of course I'd be justified in anything that came as a result.

This turns out to be a prevalent belief among Christians in America today.

Despite my comfort with gun ownership and its potential uses, there was often a nagging sense of the mental gymnastics involved in concluding this. I would come across ideas that rattled me a bit, if I were honest. Like the perspective of Gandhi, the famed Hindu leader, who once said, "The only people on earth who do not see Christ and his teachings as nonviolent are Christians." Ouch.

The reason we are so against the idea of nonviolence is that it's married to the idea of surrender. With a gun (or two) in hand, I don't have to consider surrender. I may ultimately be beaten, but

I'll have a chance to defend myself and others. Think of how many books and movies in America celebrate our military might. Even people who have never served in our military imagine themselves playing a similar role in protecting and defending others. These thoughts tend to focus much more on the power of this rather than the sacrifice that sometimes comes with this.

We assume pleasure comes from the ability to defend ourselves and others by overpowering someone else. This is a wildly popular idea. That might be an odd way to look at it, but at the very least it is a way to avoid a very non-pleasurable experience or situation. By contrast, if we consider nonviolence, it forces us to also stare surrender in the face. This is a wildly unpopular idea. But it's hard to consider community over competition while you are pointing a gun at someone.

In my own journey, I've gone from a multi-gun owner with no hesitation about using them to what is known as a kingdom pacifist (different from a political pacifist). That's been quite the transition for my own mental state and for those around me. Just this week I heard my friends talking about my change, and they referred to my gun ownership as a "fad." I joined the conversation and explained it was nothing like a fad. It wasn't that I slowly lost interest in gun ownership. Rather, I completely changed my mind about it.

Previously, I spent much time imagining what would happen if someone broke into my home. How exactly would I respond? What do I want my wife to do? What about our kids? I would think through which gun I'd get, where I'd stand, and what I'd say to the intruder. And I would hope I'd be ready in the moment. I even experienced this one time when a friend of ours set off our home alarm late one night. I was asleep when it happened, but I came fully to my senses and realized I had already taken my gun from its safe and had it in my hand. My mental practicing had paid off in the moment, and I was ready for the threat (which thankfully turned out not to be one). It was a stressful line of reasoning, but one I felt was my responsibility as the man of the house. Home defense is the issue that always tends to come up whenever nonviolence is the conversation.

Now I've changed that scenario in my mind. As a result, I'm often asked, "Would you do nothing and allow someone to harm your family or steal all of your stuff?" My answer is that I would of course do something, but my solution wouldn't be taking the other person's life.

The best analogy I've heard to understand this idea goes like this: imagine you have an aging family members (your dad, grand-father, uncle, etc.) who is mentally losing his capacity for under-standing reality. Now imagine that in one of these outbursts of confusion he comes into your home with the intent of hurting your family. He's not thinking clearly, and now your family is in danger from one of your own family members. You'd no doubt do something to stop him from doing harm. But I'm sure the idea of shooting him would be far from your mind, even if you owned a gun. Instead, you would creatively look for a way to stop the threat without harming the confused family member in the process.

Why is this analogy so helpful? Because in this analogy you aren't viewing that intruder as an enemy, but rather as a person. That's what nonviolence forces you to do. Our eager acceptance of violence, especially as Christians, causes us to dehumanize those around us in order to protect what is "ours." It should come as no surprise this is a very un-Christian thing to do. And it makes it impossible to treat people as a community.

At this point the critic thinks this is nothing more than wishful thinking. What if he can't stop an intruder without using lethal violence? The honest answer is I have to trust that God will either supernaturally protect my family in that situation or will knowingly allow harm to come to us. Either way, my stance is to be faithful to Him and allow Him to own the overall results. And in my willingness to surrender my control, I may be killed. My family may be killed, or worse. That's the worst-case scenario, and I'm not naïve to it.

> Our eager acceptance of violence ... causes us to dehumanize those around us in order to protect what is "ours." It should come as no surprise this is a very un-Christian thing to do.

But consider this: it's the exact same worst-case scenario as an eager gun owner with a willingness to use lethal force. After all, his gun could malfunction or he could be outmatched or overpowered by the intruder(s). What if a returning Navy Seal suffering from PTSD broke into his home? He may consider himself proficient with his guns, but the reality is there is no guarantee he'd be successful. In that case he's in the same position as me.

While our worst-case scenarios are identical, the difference is my best-case scenario is far greater than his.

In my best-case scenario, I might be able to talk the person out of what he intends to do. I might be able to reason with him or to stop him in another way without ending his life. For the person carrying a gun to meet an intruder, it is unlikely to end in anything other than violence.

Therefore, to argue that the only solution to a violent threat is to react in violence (and anything else is simply being passive) points to the pride of self-determination and a lack of trust in divine providence. It presupposes that there are only two alternatives: to watch violence happen or to fight violence with violence. But the evangelistic nature of our calling reminds us that God's way of acting in the face of violence was revealed in the death and resurrection of Jesus. Such an act was not simply God's way of surprising us then, but sets the framework for how we should expect God to surprise us in present and future circumstances.[4]

We see a great example of this in Jesus' response to the religious leaders of His day when they bring to Him a woman deserving punishment.[5] She had been caught in the act of adultery, a crime deserving the death penalty in their culture. The crowd gathered with rocks in their hands, ready to end her life. In our terms today, imagine each of them standing with a handgun (it would be the same purpose as why they are holding rocks). In order to trap Jesus, they deferred the question to Him. What did He recommend they do?

Their hands rested on the stones as they anticipated His response.

If Jesus told them to stone her, He would reveal Himself to be just like the religious leaders who wanted to justify themselves at the expense of others. Who wants to follow a savior like that? If Jesus told them not to stone her, He would contradict the law of Moses and jeopardize His own validity as God's Son. He might also be on the receiving end of the stoning along with this woman.

We might expect Him to reluctantly grab a rock and join in the attack of this woman. Or we might expect Him to defend her by inviting His disciples to throw rocks at the accusers. After all, we have to meet violence with equal violence, right?

Instead, Jesus masterfully pronounced that anyone who hadn't sinned, who wasn't just as guilty as the woman in question, could throw the first rock. That person could fire the first shot. Then Jesus wrote something in the dirt on the ground. He left both Himself and this woman vulnerable. Instead of an epic gunfight, the older men left first until there was no one remaining but Jesus and this woman.

That's a best-case scenario. Jesus defended others without the use of violence.

I think of the question from theologian and peace advocate Dale Aukerman: "Would God ever expect from us a mode of defense which we do not see in Jesus?"[6]

It is the belief and hope in the best-case scenario that provides pleasure. It is a tangible trust in a living God who cares deeply about my life. Often we say we trust God and then we make choices that reflect a trust only in ourselves. It is a willingness to surrender my need to achieve results at any cost.

It is the freedom from having to choose anything and everything in order to try and force results and the stress this produces. As Justin Bronson Barringer said, "True freedom is not having the right to say whatever you want without consequences; it is being able to say what is right regardless of the consequences."[7] Ironically, freedom comes from surrender. Could the living God show up in our defense today with the same creativity we saw with Jesus and the woman caught in adultery?

While this journey has caused me no shortage of scary moments and what-if questions, the surprising result is that I've gained a peace through it unlike anything else. That's because I'm not constantly worried about being strong enough, or sharp enough, or making the perfect call in that scenario. I'm not left wondering how I'd handle it if I ever did take a person's life, especially if it was over something as trivial as my TV. I've allowed myself to acknowledge that human life belongs to God and the unjust removal of life is His concern above anyone else's. I'm simply called to live as He has called me to live. That means treating everyone as human and embracing surrender when appropriate.

> While all forms of government exercise power over their subjects, citizens of the kingdom of God are to exercise power under others. That is, we are to influence others— including our enemies—by loving and sacrificially serving them. The New Testament's insistence on loving enemies and "turning the other cheek" is inseparable from this more general call and empowerment to manifest a radically unique kingdom that is "not of this world."[8]

That's how the Designer teaches us to trust Him. In return, He gives us a supernatural peace unlike anything else. We no longer stress about our own control. In surrender there is freedom and pleasure. But exploring peace through surrender and nonviolence is a complicated discussion. As Stanley Hauerwas argued, "A commitment to Christian nonviolence is not so much a position but rather a declaration that requires ongoing reflection."[9] If you want to dive deeper into nonviolence itself, I recommend you begin with the book *A Faith Not Worth Fighting For,* edited by Tripp York and Justin Bronson Barringer.

DYING TO LIVE

Perhaps the best illustration of choosing community over competition comes from Jesus' own argument about following Him. Consider the following bold words: "Whoever wants to be my disciple must deny themselves and take up their cross daily and follow me."[10] Let's break this down a bit. Let's assume you are considering becoming a disciple, a person defined by their pursuit of Jesus.

> The nature of following means we are going somewhere.
> Not staying put.
> Not simply talking about it. Not just thinking about it.
> We are following Him wherever He leads us.

Step one: deny yourself. This means acknowledging and living as if you aren't the center of the universe. You are to look at the people around you and what they need before you take care of yourself. This is an odd thing to do in our world today.

Step two: take up your cross. The cross was an instrument of horrific death the Romans devised to deter anyone from challenging them. The person to be crucified would have to carry at least part of his own cross on a journey before he was nailed to it. In fact, he was whipped prior to this in so he would be passive once the nailing began. The only rule for the Romans was to make sure the person could still carry his cross when he was done being whipped.

This would have sounded crazy when Jesus first said it. It

sounded far crazier after He went to the cross Himself. Jesus told us we don't follow Him in order to receive blessings and an easy life. Otherwise, every selfish person in the world would follow after Him and would become more selfish in the process. Rather, Jesus said we must be willing to forsake all else, even life itself, in the pursuit of following Him.

Step three: follow Him. To do this we must first ask an important question that often goes overlooked today: where is Jesus going? This isn't a question we ask one time at camp when we are in high school. This is a question that should be on our lips each morning and throughout each day. The nature of following means we are going somewhere. Not staying put. Not simply talking about it. Not just thinking about it. We are following Him wherever He leads us.

Jesus' definition of a disciple may sound like the antithesis of everything in this book thus far. At first glance it appears to be a declaration for a life of no pleasure. But if we keep reading, we see the following words after His bold three steps. This is the logic behind all of what He did and taught.

> For whoever wants to save their life will lose it, but whoever loses their life for me will save it. What good is it for someone to gain the whole world, and yet lose or forfeit their very self?[11]

If you want to save your life, if you want to force your will and your opinions and your pleasure, you'll lose it all. But when you willingly give up that selfish pursuit, you gain something else entirely that can only be gained in this way. How many people do we watch on TV or in the news who gain the whole world and lose themselves in the process?

This is the contrarian logic of pursuing pleasure. The deception of pleasure tells us we call the shots and we know best. All we need to do is follow what we want. Whatever makes us feel good. Jesus offers us something radically different: follow Him. By doing that He gives us something greater entirely.

This may seem like a huge logical contradiction. And it is. That's why those who have experienced it know it is unlike anything you get from pursuing it all for your own selfish gain.

WHAT DOES THIS SHOW US?

We've seen how pleasure comes not only through the traditional forms of sex, alcohol, or tobacco but also from the unexpected results of treating the people around us as community. Now we must consider why this is true.

The fact we find pleasure in treating others like this shows us that pleasure is much more complicated than we often assume. It goes far beyond the obvious despite the fact most of us rarely give it much thought. Pleasure turns out to be a surprisingly complicated concept. Pursuing pleasure and God isn't found only in the highlight reels for movies. It comes from the way we view the people and the experiences around us every day. By searching for pleasure through serving the people around us, we open up a limitless amount of opportunities.

It's similar to the scene Charles Dickens portrays of his crotchety character Scrooge after he finally finds a change of perspective.

He went to church, and walked about the streets, and watched the people hurrying to and fro, and patted children on the head, and questioned beggars, and looked down into the kitchens of houses, and up to the windows, and found that *everything could yield him pleasure.* He had never dreamed that any walk—that anything—could give him so much happiness.[12]

At the beginning of the book, the way Scrooge lives is about as opposite to living in community as we might ever see. The entire world is his competition. And his life is void of pleasure as a result. But Scrooge experiences a surrender-like moment where he decides to live according to a different set of values. The result is that everything provides him pleasure! What an incredible way to live everyday of our life. Scrooge learns community in one incredible night. Thankfully, this isn't an idea for classic literature alone. It's available to us now!

Are you living in a way that everything can give you pleasure?

CHAPTER TEN

MUTUALLY INCLUSIVE

PURSUING GOD
AND PLEASURE

"As we increasingly integrate our life into
the spiritual world of God, our life increasingly
takes on the substance of the eternal."

Dallas Willard

IN HIS BOOK *MORAL TRIBES*, Joshua Greene argued that we tend to misunderstand what brings us happiness. We tend to think "valuing happiness means valuing things that are directly responsible for putting smiles on our faces." I think of this as the "smile test." Think about the things that culture defines as pleasurable and we could also conclude they should put smiles on our faces. Also, consider most of what we have marketed to us. Evaluate commercials on TV or look through a print ad and you'll see an appeal to the smile test. What would be your immediate reaction if you had that? You'd smile. For items targeted at men, the image is often accompanied with smiling women as a bonus.

Immediate gratification—even at the expense of a bigger gratification later—often provides smile-worthy stimulus. That dessert we order after dinner. That vacation we take on the spur of the moment. That new car we buy on impulse. All of these bring smiles to our faces. They pass the basic smile test. But they can also quickly remove that smile if our dessert negatively affects our health or if we bury ourselves in debt for the vacation or the new car. We should approach the smile test with certain skepticism with an eye on the bigger picture. But it goes beyond that.

> In God's world, we must learn to think counterfactually and begin to make decisions that may appear odd at first, both to us and to others.

I agree with Greene on his observation on the smile test for a generally accepted definition of happiness or pleasure. And I also agree with his concern on its ultimate validity in the bigger picture. While we might say happiness begins with those things, Greene also believes it goes way beyond them. He stated the deeper reality in this way:

> What this means, at the very least, is that happiness, as a moral value, is easily misunderstood and underestimated. To think about happiness properly, one has to think abstractly and, more specifically, counterfactually. Valuing happiness, in the utilitarian sense, is not merely about valuing the things that come to mind when we think of "happiness." It's about valuing all of the things whose absence would diminish our happiness, and that includes almost everything that we value.

Thus we start to see sources of happiness all around us where once we only looked for sources of smiles. While happiness and pleasure are easy to misunderstand or underestimate, so is God.

In God's world, we must learn to think counterfactually and begin to make decisions that may appear odd at first, both to us and to others. We must learn to step outside of a culture driven by the smile test. The good decisions move us far beyond the smile test to a much deeper experience of pleasure. But how can we better make those decisions when the smile test feels so natural?

PARTY IN THE PARKING LOT

It was a typical weekday morning. I pulled into the parking lot and began the familiar walk inside. My office sat in the back of the worship center of our church. To get there I had to cross over a grass field from the parking lot. As I approached the door to our offices, I intersected one of our IT guys named David coming in at the same time. We both stopped and struck up an impromptu conversation. He stood with his back to the building, and I faced him with my back to the grass field and the parking lot.

Suddenly, mid-sentence, David shouted something to me that made no sense.

"Those guys are fighting!"

I stared at him, perplexed.

That's when I noticed he was looking past me into the parking lot. As I took a second to process his words, David took off running.

I turned around and saw two cars at one of the entrances to our parking lot. Although quite a distance from us, I witnessed two men who obviously were not thrilled with one another.

I didn't exactly have time to adequately consider my plan. David was running so I decided I should probably go help him.

Once I started running, my mind began to process the situation differently. What exactly was I going to do? What was our game plan? Were there really two men fighting in our church parking lot? As I ran, I saw a police car drive past the entrance. Surely the policeman saw the fight and was going to stop. If so, it would be a matter of moments until he used our second entrance and drove over. All I had to do was stall till then.

At some point I passed David on our run. This says less about my athletic ability and more about the fact David is shorter than I am and built like a tank.

Now I was going to be the first on the scene. As I ran closer to the men, I saw they had taken the standup disagreement to the ground. One man now sat on the other while he rained down blows to his face mixed martial arts–style. As I got closer, the amount of blood and the faces of the men both stunned me. As I looked at the two men, I saw the guy on top (doing the punching) looked to be in his fifties and the guy on bottom (receiving the punches) was probably in his sixties.

I kept running. The distance narrowed. Now I could see everything up close. I realized I had to make a decision.

My first priority was to stop the immediate violence to the man on the bottom. That meant I had to do something with the guy sitting on him. As I approached I launched a spear move on him that would make even Goldberg proud. I knocked him off the other guy and onto his back.

I didn't exactly know what to do next.

I stood there and watched as he slowly got up. Once on his feet, he approached me like I was his next target. I thought to myself, *Am I about to get in a fight in our church parking lot?*

I did my best to calm this guy down and let him know I wasn't interested in trading blows. At this point the older guy rose to his feet and was now running his mouth to my new friend. This caused him to lose interest in me and reengage the verbal assaults with his original opponent.

Moments later David arrived. With two of us there we were able to keep them separated. They both continued shouting obscenities, taunting one another, and attempting to move past David and me to get to round two. After what seemed like an eternity of this, their nerves finally calmed enough to lose some of their original interest.

You may wonder what could possibly cause two grown men to choose to get out of their vehicles and fight one another in a church parking lot. The answer? The sixty-year-old had evidently cut off the fifty-year-old on the street. Seriously?

We asked if either of them wanted us to call the police. They both declined. Evidently the thought of spending Thanksgiving week in jail was less than appealing for them. The fifty-year-old stormed off and got back in his car. As he drove away, David and I turned our attention to the older man who was bleeding profusely.

I looked around to see items of his clothing all over the parking lot. We began to gather these like we were putting Humpty Dumpty back together again. That's when he began seeing the situation more objectively.

"Thanks, guys. That could have been really bad for me."

No kidding?

That thought should probably have kept him from pulling into the parking lot in the first place, but I digress. After we made sure he was okay and was able to drive himself home, we said our good-byes.

David and I then began our long walk back to where we started our conversation. We both laughed at the absurdity of what just happened. After we reached the halfway point in our walk, I noticed a police cruiser with its lights on speeding through our parking lot.

"A little late, but now we can tell the police what happened," I said to David. I noticed he had a weird look on his face.

"No way, dude. They're going to think we were the ones fighting."

That thought had not even remotely crossed my mind. It didn't make any sense to me. We were the good guys.

The police car screeched to an abrupt halt right in front of us. Immediately, the officer opened the door and shouted, "Get your hands on the hood of the car!"

I was stunned. Was this seriously happening? I froze in place as I raced to make sense of this, unable to move.

Not David. He's from Los Angeles. In the blink of an eye David was spread-eagled, leaning on the hood of the car.

I figured this was my best option so I quickly joined him. As I glanced at my hands on the car, then at David, then at the officer, I had one of those out-of-body experiences. Suddenly I could see the whole scene play out as if from a bird's eye view. That's when the questions started flowing in.

Who's watching right now?

I imagined the paper the next day: "Local pastor arrested after bloody fight in church parking lot." *This can't be good for my career.*

At that moment I watched as our prayer pastor drove by us and waived. Evidently this didn't seem too out of the ordinary to him.

David and I began to explain calmly to the officer that we weren't the ones fighting. This took a surprising amount of convincing at first. After a while, the officer finally believed us and thanked us for what we did.

David and I then continued walking back to where we started. We went our separate ways and attempted to get to work. It didn't take long for the legend of our morning to spread like wildfire. My phone began ringing off the hook.

"Is it true? Did you guys really get in a fight in the parking lot?"

"I heard you had a run-in with the cops!"

"Did you and David fight each other?"

The story was fun to tell each time, especially to other guys. They seemed to easily imagine themselves in the story and to know exactly what they would do and how they would handle it.

When I came home from work that night, I was excited to explain it all to my wife. I had briefly mentioned earlier in the day that I had a great story for her. As I gave her the play by play, I noticed her reaction was different from everyone else I had told the story to already. She had one of those confusing looks that husbands rarely interpret correctly. I think it was a blend of concern and fear with a dash of frustration mixed in. After I finished my story, she stared at me for a moment in silence. Then she began the questions.

"What if that guy had beat you up?"

"Um, I don't know," I sheepishly replied.

"What if he had a gun?"

"He didn't."

"What if he had shot you in the face?"

"What?"

By now I was thoroughly confused. Where I saw this as a grand story of adventure, Michelle saw this as an impulsive reaction. Our shared tension shows the difficulty we have in making good decisions each day.

> Sure, some decisions we plan out, get feedback on, and then execute strategically. Others are shoved upon us and demand an immediate response.

Sure, some decisions we plan out, get feedback on, and then execute strategically. Others are shoved upon us and demand an immediate response. That's why our decision making has to be something we decide in advance. If we decide to live each day like my parking lot party, we'll be at the whim of each new circumstance we find ourselves in. But if we attempt to avoid anything like this completely, we'll find ourselves unprepared for the random moments of life.

Don't wait to decide your view on sex outside of marriage until that girl shows interest in you at the bar or club.

Don't wait to decide your view on drugs until that new friend of yours asks if you want to try some of his.

The moment for you to decide which lifestyle of pleasure you'll pick is now, as you read these words. Not later tonight when you are with your friends or at your next event. This is the idea of building into our character and making sure we choose in advance what type of life of pleasure we want.

Like Captain Chesley B. "Sully" Sullenberger, who made a

brilliant, life-saving decision in the spur of a moment, we too must prepare ourselves for what we know is to come. You may recall the amazing story of how he landed a plane of one hundred and fifty-five people onto the Hudson River after a bizarre run-in with birds in the engines.[1]

Sully became a hero in a moment.

But not really.

That's because he had long before prepared himself for a moment like that. It would be more accurate to say that all of his training and preparation prior to that flight are what made him a hero. There's no manual for this situation. "Let's see, birds-in-the-engine-over-water-with-no-time-to-think, ah yes, page forty-five." If there was a manual on what to do in a situation like that, it would be a detailed list of what Sully did. He made what proved to be the definition of a good decision.

This is our goal as well. How do we prepare now for each future moment? It will take a decision in advance. But it also takes an appreciation for the moments.

Your parking lot awaits.

WRAP IT UP

I hope by now you've seen through the illusion we often apply to spirituality and pleasure. The idea that we must choose between having fun or doing things God's way couldn't be further from the truth we see in the Bible. We can have both! We see how to find pleasure precisely *in* God's way of living.

In their book *Decisive*, Chip and Dan Heath unpack how we can make better decisions by challenging the four "villains" of decision making.

1. Narrow framing (defining our options too narrowly)
2. Confirmation bias (only looking for evidence that supports our current beliefs)
3. Short-term emotion (putting too much weight into what we feel in the moment)
4. Overconfidence (I've had success in the past so I know what I'm doing)

In order to combat these four temptations that ultimately cause us to make poor decisions, they recommend we use the WRAP process. This stands for "Widen your options. Reality-test your assumptions. Attain distance before deciding. Prepare to be wrong."

It strikes me that this is the essence of what we hope for when it comes to how we live a life of pleasure. We want to make choices that ultimately prove to be good choices. Yet when it comes to pleasure, we can struggle with each of the four villains the Heath brothers reveal.

We tend to only see pleasure with a few of our options (narrow framing). This happens when we overvalue the immediate option in front of us or when we frame it as a choice between God or pleasure.

We look for others who find pleasure in the options we see, and we use their reasoning to shore up our beliefs (confirmation bias). This often happens through the TV shows and movies we watch.

We revel in the immediate enjoyment we get from the pleasure options we choose (short-term emotion), not to mention the people we enjoy them with.

We then conclude that because we've experienced these moments of pleasure we must know what we're doing in living a life of pleasure (overconfidence). And there is often a group of others doing it with us to reinforce this.

Rarely do we realize what hangs in the balance in our everyday moments. Good decisions are often difficult to measure in the long term, let alone the short term. Life has a tendency to come at us quickly, and we usually just try our best to keep up.

PUTTING YOUR CONSTRAINTS ON GOD

How do we avoid the trap of the false choice when we are in the moment itself? If we're not careful, we can feel torn between what we want to do right now and some other thing God wants us to do. It's easy to forget these can be mutually inclusive. How do we see the bigger picture when there isn't any time left but to respond? As we saw logically, this requires breaking away from narrow framing. But we see this same argument from a spiritual point of view as well. Father J. Brian Brandsfield said,

> You're not cornered into becoming a priest or not. You're not cornered into marrying this woman or not. There are 6 billion people in the world. You're telling me that God looked at you and said, "There is only 1 thing you can do in your life, I know it and you have to guess it or else"? Could it be that you are putting your constraints on God?[2]

This logical approach to making good decisions has everything to do with how we approach God. We make the same mistakes when we choose God or pleasure exclusively. That's again why our pursuit of pleasure mirrors our pursuit of God. It's both a spiritual and logical conversation.

Specifically, to borrow Father Brian's phrase, we put our constraints on God. We often can't imagine how waiting for—or avoiding—an immediate pleasure could possibly result in greater pleasure. As a result, we usually frame the debate in our head like this:

- Should I enjoy having sex with this person on my date tonight or should I not?
- Should I have fun at this party and enjoy drinking as much as I want or should I stop after a couple drinks?
- Should I participate with my friends in this or that drug or should I pass?
- Should I enjoy looking at porn tonight or should I avoid it?
- Should I move in with my boyfriend since it makes things easier or should we continue to live separately?

From these points of view, our options are not only too limited (narrow framing) but also next to impossible to see as anything other than choosing misery for misery's sake. Left to the moment, our knee-jerk response tends to be the wrong one. But our life hangs in the balance on our answers to these questions. The quality of our sex life with our eventual spouse, our ability to enjoy alcohol later, our avoidance of dumb mistakes made while impaired, our freedom from harming others or ourselves while impaired, and our ability to fully connect with a person in marriage the rest of our life.

Some Christians then add to this that the goal of life is to simply figure out what God wants us to do or has decided for us to do. This is a spiritual version of narrow framing. God decided what you should do in this moment, so do that.

I recently overheard a bit of Christian radio in which the speaker argued that God isn't looking for volunteers. He's looking for people to obey Him. He said God doesn't want people to help Him write the script; He just wants people to do the script.

But how do we know what God wants us to do? Where is this script?

While not necessarily the Uncle Ben view of God from chapter 2, this image is equally damaging. It takes away our responsibility in the moment and leaves us only with the illusion of free will. In this view, living a life of pleasure has less to do with choosing wise options than it does with robotically obeying what you were supposed to do. Many Christians often have a hard time deciding how much God knows about or controls our life, but the Bible offers us some fascinating perspective.

Did you know the Bible shows us that God changes His mind, that God experiences regret, and that God responds according to what we pray? Biblically, we see we actually get to become coauthors of the script.

But don't worry, He's completely in control of the overall results in the process.

Thankfully, God doesn't suffer from narrow framing. The stunning view we often see in the Bible is a God who is present with us in each moment and who opens up a world of possibilities with us. Greg Boyd in *God of the Possible* said,

> Practically, a God of eternally static certainties is incapable of interacting with humans in a relevant way. The God of the possible, by contrast, is a God who can work with us to truly change what might have been into what should be.[3]

We see this in moving stories such as Hezekiah, the Israelite king who heard from God that he was about to die. Specifically, God told him, "You are going to die; you will not recover."[4] Not a lot of ambiguity there. But Hezekiah wasn't quite ready to die, so he pled with God to let him live. Didn't Hezekiah listen to the Christian radio I did and hear that he's just supposed to follow the script?

> God doesn't suffer from narrow framing. The stunning view we often see in the Bible is a God who is present with us in each moment and who opens up a world of possibilities with us.

But guess what? God changed His mind and changed reality according to what Hezekiah asked for. He gave Hezekiah fifteen more years to live.[5] Hezekiah cowrote a new script with God.

The traditional argument to this, often from legalistic Christians, is to say God knew He would eventually give Hezekiah fifteen more years to live. Makes sense, right?

As long as we are okay with a God who lies to us. Remember that whole thing about Hezekiah not recovering from his illness? Stories like Hezekiah's cause us to wrestle with a God of limitless possibilities inviting us to be coauthors of an incredible story, or having to create some serious logistical hoops to jump through.

There is example after example of this. But I'll settle for just one more to make my point here. In one of the most famous moments of the life of Jesus of Nazareth, He awaited His execution the next day by praying during the night in the Garden of Gethsemane. If you've ever heard of Jesus sweating blood, this is that scene. But the wording Jesus prayed should alert us to a bigger reality.

Faced with crucifixion, torture, and ridicule, Jesus felt appropriately overwhelmed. We read about this man, fully God and fully human, praying this prayer: "If it is possible, may this cup be taken from me." Then He added, "If it is not possible for this cup to be taken away unless I drink it, may your will be done."[6]

If it's possible?

Shouldn't Jesus know the answer to that? Yet even God in flesh interacted with God the Father in open terms. That's because God hasn't planned out every detail of your life. He's left that to you. Sure, He has a plan He'd love you to follow in order to live the type of life He designed you to live. But it's up to you. You get to decide the big picture as well as each moment.

Want to choose momentary pleasure over the bigger pleasure God intends for you?

You can.

Want to do things your way and not listen to feedback from anyone else?

You can.

Want to try life God's way and have Him join you in the process?

You can.

There are a lot of possibilities when it comes to what you choose, but not a lot of possible outcomes with each choice you make. Some will produce more pleasure than others. God in His goodness won't force His plan on your life. He's telling a bigger story throughout history, and He invites each of us to join our story to His story.

But it's our choice.

COVENANTS AND CONTRACTS

We live in a world today of contracts. It's difficult to even buy a new phone without navigating pages and pages of contractual agreements first. Or think of how many pages of contractual terms you get every time you sign up for anything (of course all read in their entirety). Contracts fuel our business interactions with those around us. Here's what you agree to, here's what I agree to, and here's what happens when one of us breaks it.

Contracts are designed to help us navigate situations where no trust exists. This is extremely helpful in these contexts. If I don't know you, I'm less likely to vulnerably trust you with something important. The danger is when we start applying contracts into areas that cannot function this way.

Consider marriage. It's a contract, right? One person vows to the other what they agree to commit to do for the rest of their life. They both promise their side of the relationship. But what happens when one person falls short of their vows? That's where contractual thinking poisons a relationship.

Sadly, for many couples this is an accurate description of their marriage. Yet this isn't the intent of marriage. We might wonder why a marriage doesn't work this way.

Because marriage is designed to be a covenant, not a contract. There's a big difference between the two. With a covenant, two parties both agree to terms like a contract. But the intent is completely different. There is a different approach in a covenant than a contract. But these are more than just differences.

Covenants and contracts are actually the opposite of each other. We might say that we enter into a contract because we fear it won't work out. Conversely, we enter into a covenant because we intend to put in the effort to make it work out. This distinction alone can make all the difference in the world in a relationship. There is a trust or there is not. Then we respond accordingly (which is why it's a bad idea to marry a person you can't trust on your wedding day).

What happens in a contractual marriage when one person falls short? Break the contract and divorce. But what happens in a covenantal marriage when one person falls short? There's no easy answer here, and that's the point. Both parties work to figure out how to restore and redeem the relationship, usually at the expense of great sacrifice. They continue to repair and build on the now-broken trust that they originally built the marriage with. All the while they work back to a position of trust.

This applies to our discussion precisely because most people attempt to follow God like a contract. This is understandable, as that's the essence of what the Old Testament law (including the Ten Commandments) was all about. If you do this, then God will bless you. If you don't, then here are the consequences to expect. This is oversimplified, as God always approaches people through a covenantal lens even if we think in terms of contract. Simply read the biblical book of Hosea to see how true this is.

But all this contractual talk in the Old Testament leads up to the full representation we see of God in Jesus, especially Jesus on the cross. Jesus invites us into a brand-new covenant of following Him. In fact, you can classify the two parts of the Bible in this way. The Old Testament is the old covenant and the New Testament is the new covenant. Not surprisingly, this new covenant is built on trust. Trust that Jesus is good and that He knows what He's talking about.

Any critical thinker will always have unresolved issues in following God. What else should we expect from a finite person following an infinite Being? But we don't follow Jesus after we have an answer to every nuanced question we could ask. We follow Jesus when we come to the place where we can trust Him. Only then do we have the proper framework to approach some of the tougher questions. Or as the apostle Paul described it, now we only see through a mirror dimly.[7]

You look for loopholes in a contract. You invest yourself for a greater good in a covenant. The difference is trust. The results are radically different. Which one describes the way in which you approach God?

MATTRESSES, MONEY, AND MISPERCEPTIONS

Recently my wife and I began shopping for a new mattress. We thought we'd hit up a few stores to get a feel for what's out there. At our first stop we immediately had a greeter start a conversation with us as we entered. She had a bizarre, passive-aggressive style. When she asked us what we were looking for, we replied that we were pretty open and were shopping for something that fit us. Her answer was that if we didn't know what we wanted, then she couldn't help us. She then led us to the mattress section and walked away.

I was surprised and bothered at the same time. Worse yet, the greeter watched us from a distance. Now, I only worked sales for a few years of my life, but I'm pretty sure that when you get an open-minded customer, you take that opportunity to guide them to something they will fall in love with. Not happening with our lady.

I looked at Michelle as we walked out and said, "That was weird, right?" She agreed.

We walked a few stores down to another mattress store. At this one, we saw a salesman again as soon as we entered. He was coming from somewhere in the back, and after he said hi to us he sat down at a desk up front. The rest of the conversation we had with him—in which we asked him a few questions—consisted only of him responding to our questions without making eye contact. He just continued to stare at his screen. We decided it was time to go again.

> We follow Jesus when we come to the place where we can trust Him. Only then do we have the proper framework to approach some of the tougher questions.

I looked at Michelle as we walked out and said, "I'm done shopping for mattresses. Let's get dinner."

As we reflected on this bizarre chain of experiences, Michelle made a telling observation. "They don't think we have money." As soon as she said it I realized that was it. We were young, dressed casually, and probably looked a bit sleep-deprived (and we didn't even have our four kids with us). But as a middle-class white guy, who has always been a middle-class white guy, I'm a bit embarrassed to admit I'm not used to this feeling, especially as extreme as we experienced it.

But here's the irony: we had saved the money to buy any bed in either of these stores with cash. And I didn't have a specific bed in mind to limit our options. A good salesperson could have had an ideal customer on their hands.

But we evidently didn't look the part.

So in an area built on commission and snap judgments, we were deemed not worth the time. This is a tough pill to swallow, especially when you know it's not accurate. Selfishly, I wanted to walk back into each store and explain to them what they had just missed out on (I'm told this is a *Pretty Woman* moment). But it doesn't take long to play out that scenario to realize how petty it ultimately sounds. So instead, I've tried to make this a learning moment for myself.

We all make the same mistake our mattress salespeople made. We make snap decisions that affect the way we treat people around us. And like those salespeople, we risk losing opportunities. Even worse, in our more sinister moments we may even work to keep others from experiencing pleasure themselves. Ever rooted for someone not to succeed or celebrated when something bad happened to them? Left to the moment we can make decisions that will end up keeping ourselves or others from pleasure.

That's why we should approach the snap decisions we make about pleasure and God with a certain level of skepticism. Sometimes our gut leads us in the right direction. Often it doesn't. That's why smart decisions come with a regular amount of scrutiny and evaluation. Yet how many of us take the time to genuinely consider what our choices bring us *and* what they exclude us from?

Our choices matter. So does our ability to make the right one. Tragically, many people make thousands of choices in their lives constantly picking between pleasure or God. Yet when we choose pleasure apart from God, we see but a glimpse of the real thing. Not to mention we experience life without God. But when we look for true pleasure, we find not only the fullness of pleasure but also the person who designed it.

God won't force you to choose Him or His design of pleasure. Yet don't believe that all options are equal. We don't need to settle for one when both is an option.

CHAPTER ELEVEN

THE PLEASURE
OF CHOICE

PURSUING GOD
AND FINDING HIM

"You make known to me the path of life;
you will fill me with joy in your presence,
with eternal pleasures at your right hand."

Psalm 16:11

THE GREATER OUR IMMEDIATE PLEASURE, the less we long for a
fulfillment from something else and the less we look forward to
even greater delayed pleasures to come, especially in eternity. When
heaven sounds like a demotion, we should realize our momentary
pleasure has taken the wheel and is driving our car.

Is this all there is? Is the immediate pleasure the only pleasure
that really matters? In Epicurus's letter to Herodotus, he expressed
concern that pleasure must only exist in the here and now.

It is not possible to imagine the soul existing and having
sensation without the body, and experiencing these movements when there no longer exists that which encloses and
surrounds the soul, in which it now exists and has these
movements.

As a result of these beliefs, Dante assigned space for Epicurus in the sixth circle of hell in his book *Inferno*. That's a disappointing end for our friend Epicurus, but the beliefs he taught are even more disappointing. Even if we experienced the fullness of pleasure now, if it ends once we die, then that means there is a short shelf-life for pleasure. If, however, it continues into eternity, then the road we take toward pleasure matters greatly.

Sadly, most people live for the pleasure of the moment at the expense of the pleasure of the future.

We see this in the many items we go into debt to buy. But we also see how this immediate need for pleasure detracts from future pleasure in areas like premarital sex and drinking alcohol to excess. But it goes even further. Each of us must ask ourselves a critical question.

Is this all there is?

Are the atheists right when they argue that death is nothing more than returning to the nothingness we "experienced" before we were alive? Or is it possible the idea of heaven could be a reality?

You get to a point eventually when you come to see the Bible is either intrinsically true, including even those passages you can't make sense out of yet, or a fairy-tale story. My experience has taught me that what the Bible says adds up. As a result, I'm left to believe this life is a precursor for another life. Not an endless series of lives, as reincarnation teaches, but two lives: an earthly life and an eternal life.

I believe there are two possibilities when you die. One involves eternity in the pleasure of the completeness of God, and the other is void of God and His pleasure. If pleasure is my goal, I should spend my years in this life heading further down the road, or closer to, an eternity of pleasure. It would be tragic to miss an eternity of pleasure because I opted for a few years of it on earth instead.

Too often we miss the experience of the five-course meal because we filled up on a candy bar from a vending machine in the lobby.

Imagine if you could rate your life's current pleasure on a scale from one to ten, with ten being the most enjoyable life a person could live. What number would you assign your life? I invite you to pause a moment and give yourself a number before you keep reading.

If your number is low, it's time to try something else. Your methods for arriving at pleasure aren't working. If you have lived contrary to the logic we've discussed in this book, I'd encourage you to try pleasure differently. As my dad is fond of saying, nothing changes when nothing changes.

If your number is high, does it put you on the trajectory to experience a life of pleasure after this life? Said differently, does your current pursuit of pleasure come at the expense of future pleasure or is it a preview of greater pleasure yet to come?

Are you content with your number? Could you imagine life with a higher number? Now could you imagine unending life for eternity with a higher number?

Until heaven is an appealing idea for us, we will always pursue immediate pleasure at the expense of the future.

Is this all there is? Because if it isn't, we better make sure we don't sacrifice the future for the present. But here's the best part: we might expect that to receive pleasure in eternity we must forego it in this life. But in Christ, just the opposite is true! Finding pleasure in God's design in this life takes us down the road to finding pleasure for eternity. But it also means we can miss experiencing real pleasure in both as well.

LOREM IPSUM

You have probably seen text on a website or graphic that begins with "*Lorem ipsum dolor sit amet.*" It's the beginning of a Latin text commonly used as a placeholder for sample text. You'll see it on new websites or page layouts for preview. It has been used for this purpose since the 1500s. While most of us have seen it, few know what it means.

The text comes from a book called *The Extremes of Good and Evil* written by Cicero in 45 BC. In the year 1914, H. Rackham translated the first part of the text as follows:

> But I must explain to you how all this mistaken idea of denouncing pleasure and praising pain was born and I will give you a complete account of the system, and expound the actual teachings of the great explorer of the truth, the master-builder of human happiness. No one rejects, dislikes, or avoids pleasure itself, because it is pleasure, but because those who do not know how to pursue pleasure rationally encounter consequences that are extremely painful.

How surprising that the sample text we use today for all manner of purposes is a two-thousand-year-old passage about the difficulty of finding pleasure. Yet we shouldn't be surprised. Indeed, pursuing pleasure rationally is the same search we have today. And we still wish to avoid consequences that are extremely painful.

Our search connects us with generations before us, but it forces a question: Will we ever find what we are looking for? Will we join men like Cicero and Epicurus in struggling continuously to find the right way to experience pleasure?

We don't have to. It's possible to pursue pleasure rationally, but it depends how much we can break from the norm to find it.

It's a waste of your time to search for something that has already been found.

NORMAL IS BROKEN

The best sign of whether this book will launch you on your pleasure journey is whether you are content with normal. By definition, most of us are.

It's normal to expect decreased pleasure.

It's normal to accept consequences from pleasure.

It's normal to search for pleasure without a clear sense of how to get it.

I think something is wrong with normal.

But normal doesn't get you any weird looks. It doesn't cause anyone to challenge your beliefs. And it certainly doesn't cause you to stand out. Many people content themselves with normal.

If you look up the word *norm* in the dictionary, you find two different variations of definitions.[1] One definition, I suspect the older definition, says norm is "a principle of right action binding upon the members of a group and serving to guide, control, or regulate proper and acceptable behavior." The other (more common) way we use it as "something (such as a behavior or way of doing something) that is usual or expected."

I think we need to go back to the old definition of normal, focusing not just what most people are doing but what actually produces the right results we crave. It all depends on how badly we want to experience pleasure. Not the fleeting impulse, but a lingering lifestyle. Epicurus made his position clear: "I spit on the beautiful and those who idly gawk at it, if it produces no pleasure."

"I spit on the beautiful"?

That's not normal.

I imagine Epicurus as a weird guy with a healthy dose of social awkwardness. He'd likely be the guy you'd run into at a party while you're on your way to get a drink. He'd corner you with some bizarre topic of conversation, and you'd try to find a way out and give the secret signal to a friend to come and save you.

We've all been there.

Or he might have been more like the main character from the movie *A Beautiful Mind*, someone you know to be brilliant but can't quite seem to connect with.

Try to imagine the way someone would sound saying, "I spit on the beautiful." It sounds crazy.

Personally, I like the beautiful. I probably even gawk at it occasionally. But that's what it takes to break out of normal. Sadly, even though Epicurus had the drive covered, his aim was off.

Normal is lifeless Christianity. Jesus offers us more. He offers us an experience that defies what is usual or expected.

I think of the story in Lois Lowry's book *The Giver*. I've always found this story so moving, even though I'm not entirely sure why. It tells about a society without emotion, feelings, and memories. Instead, they've designated one individual called the Receiver to handle all of that on behalf of the community. When it's time to select a new Receiver, the current Receiver changes roles and becomes the Giver. The conversations between the Giver and this young new Receiver named Jonas are poignant and inspiring. As Jonas learns about things like color for the first time, we get a moving glimpse at the excitement he begins to feel.

"It happened," Jonas said. "It happened to the books, but it went away again."

"I'm right then," The Giver said. "You're beginning to see the color red."

"The what?"

The Giver sighed. "How to explain this? Once, back in the time of the memories, everything had a shape and size, the way things still do, but they also had a quality called *color*. There were a lot of colors, and one of them was called red. That's the one you are starting to see."

Jonas struggles to comprehend the significance of what he's just learned. The world isn't black and white? There's a red color? There are more colors too? He attempts to give words to this new revelation.

"It was so—oh, I wish language were more precise! The red was so beautiful!"

The Giver nodded. "It is."

"Do you see it all the time?"

"I see all of them. All the colors."

"Will I?"

"Of course. When you receive the memories. You have the capacity to see beyond. You'll gain wisdom, then, along with colors. And lots more."

I find this conversation so touching because this has been my experience discovering a God who is truly good; in fact, good beyond my wildest imagination. And a God who instructs me on how to live this life so I don't have to wander around or figure it all out myself. It is the feeling of "seeing beyond" for ourselves. Where we once saw only black and white, we begin to see color. Maybe, just maybe, there is more to pleasure than we ever thought possible.

> I find this conversation so moving because this has been my experience discovering a God who is truly good; in fact, good beyond my wildest imagination.

But I also acknowledge how not normal this ends up being for most people. Most of the world doesn't see red like this, both in their view of God and their view of pleasure. That's why this conversation matters to me as much as it does. Once you've seen colors, you want others to see them too. I want others to realize Uncle Ben is a character for a cartoon and not an accurate portrayal of the God we find in the Bible. I want others to realize pleasure doesn't have to come with the consequences and ill effects we've come to accept. There's a better way.

But it requires us to *see beyond* that which we call normal.

THE POWER OF IDEAS

Our ideas matter, especially our ideas of God.

Let's break it down logically for a moment. If I assume that those hot and fresh-off-the-conveyor-belt doughnuts from Krispy Kreme have ingredients that will allow me to live a healthy lifestyle and feel great, I'm going to have an issue. This is especially true for the Krispy Kreme cheeseburger, affectionately known as "baseball's best burger."[2]

If I relegate seat belts as a waste of time, I'm going to put my life and the lives of my family at unnecessary risk. At a minimum, I'm inviting an easily avoidable ticket.

If I assume that country music is actually *good* music, I'm going to experience a lot of depression and confusion. (This is a running joke with many of my Arizona friends. It's tough growing up in Arizona when you don't happen to be a fan of country music.)

If I assume that cows are holy and could be a person reincarnated (as Hindus believe), I will drive around a cow instead of moving it from the middle of the street. As an entire community, we will stop traffic for a cow until it moves. I've seen this happen in Nepal firsthand.

The list goes on and on. Ideas shape actions.

Cultures create constitutions based on values and beliefs. These shape the governments, which enforce the principles established. This is evident in the laws of that culture that ensure people live according to the agreed ideas. A revolution is a moment in history when the people decide they need new ideas to live by.

In the biblical book of Jonah, God called Jonah to go and

preach to the city of Nineveh. Nineveh was a great city of antiquity and was then the dominant city of the region. God had a heart for the Ninevites and Jonah didn't. In fact, Jonah cared so little about them he tried everything possible to avoid bringing them healing and forgiveness through God. God eventually persuaded Jonah to obey Him (ever heard that story of the big fish?), and Jonah told the Ninevites to turn from their wicked ways. And then the remarkable happened. The entire city altered its course. They turned from the wicked things they were doing and embraced what God wanted them to do. Jonah was one of the most successful prophets of all time.

But the story doesn't end there.

That's why I love reading the Bible. There is so much humanity represented authentically. Jonah then turned on God because God forgave the city of Nineveh. Instead of Jonah changing his heart about the Ninevites, as they did with God, Jonah vented his frustration to God and told him he was so angry he wanted to die. Not exactly your model prophet of God. We learn an incredible insight about God from the last verse of the book of Jonah. In verse 11 of chapter 4, in response to all of Jonah's whining, God asked him, "Should I not have concern for the great city of Nineveh, in which there are more than a hundred and twenty thousand people who cannot tell their right hand from their left?"

God pointed out the depravity of the Ninevites to Jonah. He used an incredible phrase—"people who cannot tell their right hand from their left"—to sum up an entire culture of belief leading to brokenness. It wasn't just one person's belief, because beliefs aren't private. There were a hundred and twenty thousand people who held the same values. God told Jonah that He needed him to help them change their ideas. And we see that when they changed their shared ideas, they changed their city's history.

In the 1800s, a German poet named Heinrich Heine said, "Thought precedes action as lightning precedes thunder."[3] The things we think about lead to the things we do. That's why our beliefs, as theoretical as we might think they are, translate quickly into actions. It's ironic that he made these statements in Germany, roughly one hundred years before Hitler would usher in radical ideas with radical results. Heine is perhaps best known for his quote, found in a few of the major Holocaust museums, about how when people burn books they will eventually burn people. It comes as no surprise that his own books were among those that Hitler burned.

Ideas have consequences.

It is tempting to argue, at some point in this journey, "What does it matter what I think about pleasure?" The answer, readily clear with perspective, is everything. You pursue pleasure according to what you believe about pleasure.

If you decide you can experience pleasure on your own terms and in your own ways, you will also experience many consequences that decrease each pleasure. Welcome to normal. But if you decide there is a right way and a wrong way to experience pleasure, you will spend time trying to get the most out of pleasure without the unnecessary consequences.

But this argument falls far short of political correctness. Shouldn't we allow everyone to draw their own conclusions about pleasure? What does it matter if they live according to ideas far different from mine?

If ideas have consequences, both good and bad, then none of

us are immune from the ideas of others. Even Austin Cline, a leading voice for atheism today and a person whom we might expect to push on the notion of proper belief, argued the same point.

> Beliefs are important because behavior is important and your behavior depends on your beliefs. Everything you do can be traced back to beliefs you hold about the world . . . All this means that beliefs are not an entirely private matter.[4]

Our best chance is to start with the right beliefs about God and His creation of pleasure. These would be healthy beliefs that lead to maximum pleasure. Any unhealthy belief that deviates from God's design decreases the pleasure we'd experience. The further we move away from the design, the more brokenness we'll experience in our pursuit of pleasure. But the reverse is also true. The closer we align ourselves to the design, the more complete our pleasure will be.

If we can conclude that God is indeed good, and that God created pleasure, then it stands to reason that pleasure is inherently good, or at least can be enjoyed in a good way. We are searching for a good part of creation from a good God. So why is pleasure so often not good?

THE BOTTOM LINE

We are all pursuing pleasure, whether we realize it or not. And each of us takes a different route to arrive at our pleasure. As we've seen throughout this book, there are multiple ways to look at this, and the Bible offers one way that often runs contrary to what we hear in the culture around us. Once we've heard the arguments and considered the logic for ourselves, we must each answer a question.

Can I trust Jesus enough to obey Him?

Throughout my own experience and watching the experiences of countless people around me, I am convinced there is a reason why God instructs us to live a certain way. It has nothing to do with keeping us from pleasure but rather showing us how to experience the true depths of pleasure.

In his *Principal Doctrines*, Epicurus argued, "No pleasure is evil in itself; but the means of obtaining some pleasures bring in their wake troubles many times greater than the pleasures." This is a reality each generation must accept. While the specific ways in which we enjoy pleasures can change through the years, our need for pleasure and the design of these pleasures never change.

Our goal is not to experience the troubles that come with pleasure that Epicurus references. Yet that's precisely what happens when we follow pleasure on our terms. We may think we know best. Jesus suggested otherwise.

Can we trust God enough to pursue pleasure the way He describes it? Can we get past the Uncle Ben view of a tyrant god to the God of the Bible who created pleasure?

If your life has been defined by a radically different reality than what I've described in this book, I invite you to look for a new perspective. This is found in the words of the Bible and in Christian community. Like anything else, it can be daunting to start when you don't know where to begin. The great news is there is likely a church community near you where you can meet others pursuing a life of pleasure God's way. And the Bible is available at your fingertips to learn more. I'd encourage you to download the YouVersion Bible app right now and begin reading the book of John in the

New Testament.[5] The app is free, and it allows you to easily navigate through God's Word.

There's a better story for you to join.

IT'S NEVER TOO LATE

Let's say you've come to some new realizations through reading this book. You've seen a different life is available to you if you change the way you make decisions. That's exciting.

But that might also bring with it a feeling that you are late to the party. That you are too far gone. That this would have been great news a few years ago. It's easy to feel the weight of bad decisions and believe they are irreversible.

It's never too late.

It's never too late to pursue true pleasure in the present moment. It's never too late to admit you don't want to continue down a road that is taking you somewhere you don't want to go. The Bible calls this idea repentance. It happens when we acknowledge that if we don't like where we are headed, the most progressive move we can make is to turn around completely and walk the other direction.

> No matter how you got here, now you need to figure out where to go next. The incredible thing about the biblical God is that He enjoys redeeming broken lives. It's kind of His thing.

The philosopher Walter Kaufman once said, "It makes for a better life if one has a rendezvous with death." Those types of rendezvous have a way of bringing a unique perspective. Every bad decision you've made in the past can be a catalyst for you to make different decisions in the future. The point is that no matter how you got here, now you need to figure out where to go next.

The incredible thing about the biblical God is that He enjoys redeeming broken lives. It's kind of His thing. He once took a guy named Saul, who was killing the early Christians, and transformed him into one of the greatest leaders the church has ever seen. God even changed his name to the man we know today as the apostle Paul. Because of his own journey and the perspective that came with it, Paul would write about the transformation God wants to do in our lives as well. In a letter to the church in Corinth, the apostle Paul wrote, "Therefore, if anyone is in Christ, the new creation has come: The old has gone, the new is here!"[6]

It's never too late.

When you decide to pursue pleasure God's way, you immediately begin to notice the change. It doesn't mean your kids will start behaving, your job will stop frustrating you, you'll be immune from tragedy, or all your problems will vanish into thin air. But it means you'll live with something new available to you. As another biblical writer named Titus said,

> For the grace of God has appeared that offers salvation to all people. It teaches us to say "No" to ungodliness and worldly passions, and to live self-controlled, upright and godly lives in this present age.[7]

Many people think of grace as the get-out-of-jail-free card. And it is. That happens when we live by what Jesus Christ did on our behalf by dying on a cross in our place for our mistakes.

But Titus shows us it's so much more.

Grace teaches us how to live and how to make decisions that will lead us to a life of pleasure. This happens when we turn over the control of calling the shots. It happens when we reverse what Adam and Eve did in the garden. We let God know He gets to decide good and evil in our life. The apostle Peter described this process by explaining we make an exchange in our nature.

> His divine power has given us everything we need for a godly life through our knowledge of him who called us by his own glory and goodness. Through these he has given us his very great and precious promises, so that through them you may participate in the divine nature, having escaped the corruption in the world caused by evil desires.[8]

When we follow Jesus, He gives us His Spirit, which allows us to join in the divine nature. Talk about life-changing! We no longer have to struggle to avoid the troubles pleasure brings on our own. We have a guide sent from the Designer Himself.

So if you are late to the party, worry not. But I also don't want to cause Christians who are reading this to feel that somehow they showed up too early to the party. We all want to feel a part of the action, and the amazing news is that the rewards are available to each of us.

Jesus told a story[9] about a landowner who needed work done on his property. Early in the morning he recruited people to help him and offered to pay them a day's wage. Realizing there was more work to do, the landowner went back out at nine in the morning and recruited more people. He offered to pay them what was fair. He did the same thing later in the day and recruited more people at noon, three in the afternoon, and five in the evening.

Common logic here would warrant that the early workers would make more than those hired later in the day. Whatever scale the landowner used, most of us would agree there should be some type of scale used. Yet in Jesus' story, at the end of the day the landowner paid everyone the same wage!

As you might imagine, the initial workers protested this. The landowner asked why it was wrong for him to pay everyone what he thought was fair. After all, everyone made what they agreed to work for. This isn't a story about an unfair God. It's a story about how easily we feel jealousy of those around us.

The point of the story is that every worker made a day's wages. Sure, some of them worked less time. But all of them were able to enjoy the reward.

But it's more than an interesting story.

This story is tangibly reenacted in the lives of people like Jeffrey Dahmer. Dahmer was a serial killer convicted of brutally killing more than seventeen people. In fact, if you research the details of the killings, it will likely turn your stomach and stir up emotions of anger and disgust. He was eventually sentenced to fifteen life terms and was later killed by another inmate in prison. It's a horrific story all around.

What you may not know is that Jeffrey Dahmer accepted Christ while in prison. Shortly before he died, the man who unleashed untold amounts of pain to dozens of people's lives was forgiven by the God of the universe. The minister who baptized him, Roy Ratcliff, is often asked about the nature of Dahmer's faith. He said,

One of the most common questions put to me about Jeff has to do with the sincerity of his faith. And I usually hear this from Christians. They ask if Jeff was truly sincere in his desire for baptism and in his Christian life. My answer is always the same: Yes, I am convinced he was sincere.[10]

Jeffrey Dahmer was the worker who was hired at five in the afternoon yet still received a full day's wages.

Depending on your own journey with God, that's either an extreme encouragement for what God continues to offer you, or an extreme frustration based on how you've lived thus far.

It's not too late.

But it's not too early either.

We can also conclude Jeffrey Dahmer isn't the target life we'd choose to imitate. While Dahmer met Christ before his death, the fact is he didn't have the opportunity to know Him long before he met Him for eternity. I doubt he would have described his life as a good one.

If God really is offering me a life of pleasure, why would I not try to enjoy it as much as possible in this life now? The early workers were able to be with the landowner on his property all day. What better place to be?

Jesus taught the same concept in another story[11] about a father with two sons. The younger son took his half of the inheritance and squandered it in wild living. The older son stuck around and continued to work for the father. Eventually, the younger son returned, and instead of getting a reprimand from his father, he was received with a party. Everyone was thrilled he was back . . . except his older brother. All his older brother could see was that it was not fair. That's why Roy Ratcliff said he's asked about the validity of Dahmer's faith primarily from Christians.

Whether you experience God early in your life or at the very end, Jesus' offer remains the same. There's a party going on, and He wants us all to be a part of it. Some people experience this early in life and must fight the temptation to feel they've earned it. Others experience it later in life and wonder how things could have been different if they'd done it earlier.

Either way, God wants us with Him. Jesus told story after story to convince us of this fact. Jud Wilhite said in *Pursued*,

> Yet the greatest, most pleasurable, most enjoyable experience of any person is to be able to know God, relate to Him, and make much of Him. There is nothing else that compares with this experience. Nothing even comes close to being able to have a life with the God and Creator of the universe. This is the peak of the mountain of pleasure. This is what we were designed for.

THE FAVOR OF GOD

I want to close this book by explaining one of the things I regularly pray for. I regularly ask for God's favor to be in my life. I ask for it over my family and my career, over the book you are reading. Call it God's blessing or any other term you like. But the idea is that I want my life marked by something greater than myself. C. S. Lewis summed it up beautifully in *The Weight of Glory*:

Our Lord finds our desires not too strong, but too weak. We are half-hearted creatures, fooling about with drink and sex and ambition when infinite joy is offered us, like an ignorant child who wants to go on making mud pies in a slum because he cannot imagine what is meant by the offer of a holiday at the sea. We are far too easily pleased.

I don't want to miss *great* because I settled for *good enough*.

That's the choice we each make daily. When we decide we can achieve pleasure on our terms, we settle for good enough. When we submit to God's way of finding pleasure, and the favor that follows, we experience a life that exceeds our greatest expectations.

Epicurus spent his personal and professional life pursuing pleasure.

Every person who has ever lived pursues it in one way or another.

But not every person actually experiences a life of pleasure. The act of pursuing pleasure does not grant it. Only through pursuing pleasure as designed do we ever fully taste it.

I wish for you to be unique. For you to live with the favor of God's design. For you to not be too easily pleased. And for you to know pleasure.

ACKNOWLEDGMENTS

When I was in high school, my girlfriend created a drawing for me of the aspirations I had for my life. Pictures of my young bucket list flowed around the page. One image was a book cover with the title *The Deception of Pleasure*. My teenage book idea would one day grow up to be the book you now hold in your hands. And I would grow up to marry that amazing woman.

To my beautiful wife, Michelle, thank you. For dreaming, for believing, and for balancing just the right amount of feedback to keep me going without ever letting any of it go to my head. Thanks for being flexible and growing with me. I viewed life very differently before we were married, and you've taken each new perspective in stride. You are a joy to do life with. God blessed you with a loving heart and a tenacious spirit. And I get to enjoy both.

To our bounty of little people: Gavin, Madsen, Adelyn, and little A: I love you. You demand more of me than I realized I could offer, but I'm better for it. I would choose you again every day. I pray you take these ideas further than I ever could. The world needs people like you.

A big thanks to my parents, Cal and Lisa, for the lifetime of support they continue to give me, and for instilling in me the fact I make them proud. Thanks for giving me a head start. The odds were stacked in my favor with you two as parents. You have been faithful with much, and your legacy continues to grow.

Thanks to all my extended family who do life with us day in and day out. It's been said it takes a village to raise a child, but I've found it also takes a village to raise a dream. Thanks for being a family we actually like to spend time with.

Thanks to Central Christian Church Arizona for giving me a position where I can lead and be led in so many creative ways. It's an amazing culture. Many of the ideas in this book came of age in this community, especially our life group.

To my agent, Don Gates, a man who helped bring these words to life through his determination and skill. When I felt like throwing in the towel, you made magic happen. You have made this experience one filled with pleasure instead of pain.

Thanks to the team at Worthy Publishing, particularly Jeana, Leeanna, and Kyle. Kyle, you've done an amazing job as editor making sure the craziness in my head makes some sort of sense by the time it hits the page.

I'm also blessed by a community of voices who spoke into this book at different points along the way and allowed it to take its final shape. Guys like Curtis Holtzen, Justin Narducci, Brad Zehring, Paul Carpenter, and Chris Hedrick. Thanks also to all of the people who put their name behind this project with an endorsement. I appreciate the chance to stand on your shoulders. To Greg Boyd, for pushing my theology and helping me to see past my own cultural biases. You've been an incredible mentor and friend to me.

A special shout-out to Starbucks store 5966. This book was fueled by your iced coffee and power outlets. You run a great district, Tricia.

I could fill a book simply with my appreciation for the countless people who bless my life on a daily basis. Community is messy . . . and worth it.

Thanks.

NOTES

Prologue

1. James Gorman, "Mice Run for Fun, Not Just Work, Research Shows," www.nytimes.com (May 20, 2014).

Chapter 1

1. Alice Robb, "92 Percent of College Students Prefer Reading Print Books to E-Readers," www.newrepublic.com (January 14, 2015).
2. Blaise Pascal, *Pensées* (Thoughts), 3:65.
3. Tim Teeman, "'I Think I Kill Pleasure': Philip Seymour Hoffman Reflects on His Children, and Facing Life and Death," www.thedailybeast.com (June 3, 2014).
4. Daniel Burke, "Millennials Leaving Church in Droves, Study Finds," www.cnn.com (May 14, 2015).
5. Eugene O'Connor, *The Essential Epicurus* (Amherst, NY: Prometheus Books, 1993).
6. N. T. Wright, *Paul and the Faithfulness of God: Book One* (Minneapolis: Fortress Press, 2013).
7. http://dictionary.reference.com/browse/ataraxia, accessed July 7, 2015.
8. Genesis 2:17
9. Genesis 2:17 EXB
10. "Selected Fragments by Epicurus," translated by Peter Saint-Andre, www.monadnock.net/epicurus/fragments.html (2011), accessed July 7, 2015.

Chapter 2

1. David Dark, *The Sacredness of Questioning Everything* (Grand Rapids, MI: Zondervan, 2009), 10.
2. *The Office*, Season Two, "The Fight."
3. http://www.snopes.com/politics/religion/drlaura.asp, accessed July 7, 2015.
4. Deuteronomy 5:12–15
5. Exodus 31:14–15
6. Numbers 15:32–36
7. Deuteronomy 4:37–38
8. Genesis 37:35; Numbers 16:30–33; Ecclesiastes 9:10; Psalm 86:13; Ezekiel 31:15; Job 10:21
9. Hades, Gehenna, and Tartarus
10. This incorporates aspects of Christian mortalism or "soul sleep."
11. Christopher M. Date, Gregory G. Stump, and Joshua W. Anderson, editors, *Rethinking Hell: Readings in Evangelical Conditionalism* (Eugene, OR: Wipf and Stock Publishers, 2014), xii.
12. See Hebrews 11.

13. 2 Corinthians 5:19
14. Colossians 2:15
15. Hebrews 2:14
16. Greg Boyd, "The 'Christus Victor' View of the Atonement," www.reknew.org (January 8, 2008).
17. Hosea 13:14
18. "A Tough Question," www.tomorrowsreflection.com (June 26, 2013).
19. I've edited these for grammatical purposes.
20. 1 Corinthians 15:14

Chapter 3

1. Genesis 1:26a NLT
2. Augustine, *On Christian Teaching*, 3.37.
3. John 10:11–18
4. Genesis 4:2
5. Genesis 46:31–34, emphasis added.
6. Many people think of David as the second king of Israel, but Saul's son Ish-Bosheth was actually second. See 2 Samuel 3:6–21.
7. 2 Samuel 7:8
8. Zephaniah 2:5–6
9. Amos 7:14–15
10. Ezekiel 34:1–6
11. Psalm 23:6, emphasis added.
12. Isaiah 58:11
13. John 10:10
14. Unless otherwise noted, all Epicurus quotes taken from *The Essential Epicurus* (Amherst, NY: Prometheus Books, 1993).

Chapter 4

1. Scott Sauls, "Thoughts on Sex," www.scottsauls.com (January 29, 2015).
2. Hebrews 13:4
3. John 8:44
4. Matthew 19:6
5. Jason DeParle, "Two Classes, Divided by 'I Do,'" www.nytimes.com (July 14, 2012).
6. Edward O. Laumann, John H. Gagnon, Robert T. Michael, and Stuart Michaels, *The Social Organization of Sexuality: Sexual Practices in the United States* (Chicago: University of Chicago Press, 1994).
7. Lee Ann Obringer, "How Love Works," www.howstuffworks.com.
8. "Oxytocin Modulates Social Distance Between Males and Females," www.jneurosci.org (November 14, 2012).
9. www.xxxchurch.com/stats/men, accessed July 7, 2015.
10. Donald L. Hilton, Jr., and Clark Watts, "Pornography Addiction: A Neuroscience Perspective," www.ncbi.nlm.nih.gov (February 21, 2011).

11. Scott Christian, "The Brain Scan That Will Tell If You're Addicted to Porn," www.GQ.com (September 23, 2013).

12. AsapSCIENCE, "The Science of Pornography Addiction," https://www.youtube.com/watch?v=1Ya67aLaaCc#t=35, accessed July 7, 2015.

13. Jason Chen, "Finally, Some Actual Stats on Internet Porn," www.gizmodo.com (June 1, 2010); graphics originally from www.OnlineMBA.com, but no longer accessible there.

14. Cole Nesmith, "The Dangers of Emotional Pornography," www.relevantmagazine.com (December 28, 2010).

15. Anahad O'Connor, "The Claim: Swallowed Gum Takes a Long Time to Digest," www.newyorktimes.com (August 28, 2007).

16. Scott Christian, "10 Reasons Why You Should Quit Watching Porn," www.GQ.com (November 20, 2013).

17. Ed Stetzer, "Rick Warren Interview on Muslims, Evangelism & Missions," www.ChristianityToday.com (March 2, 2012).

18. Matthew 19:1–12; Mark 10:1–12

19. Brent Pickett, "Homosexuality," *The Stanford Encyclopedia of Philosophy,* http://plato.stanford.edu/entries/homosexuality/, accessed July 7, 2015.

20. "Episode 20—LGBTQ," The Liturgist Podcast, www.theliturgists.com (May 19, 2015).

21. See Romans 6:1–2.

22. http://tomorrowsreflection.com/wp-content/uploads/2009/04/kimerone28099s-story.pdf, accessed July 7, 2015.

23. Marlow Stern, "Gay No More: The Story of Michael Glatze," www.thedailybeast.com (February 2, 2015).

24. Luke 24:13–35

25. Elizabeth Dias, "Nashville Evangelical Church Comes Out for Marriage Equality," www.time.com (January 29, 2015).

Chapter 5

1. Proverbs 31:4–7

2. 1 Corinthians 11:20–21

3. Acts 2:16

4. The Q Conference, www.qideas.org.

5. 1 Timothy 5:23

6. Matthew 11:18–19

7. Stephen Mansfield, *The Search for God and Guinness* (Nashville: Thomas Nelson, 2009), 6–7.

8. Examples found in Warren W. Wiersbe's *Walking with the Giants* (Grand Rapids, MI: Baker Book House, 1976).

Chapter 6

1. www.dictionary.reference.com

2. Genesis 2:15

3. Genesis 2:19

4. Genesis 3:23

5. Genesis 3:18–19a

6. Igniter Media, "The Marshmallow Test," https://www.youtube.com/watch?v=QX_oy9614HQ, accessed July 7, 2015.

7. John Lassiter, "Tricks to Animating Characters with a Computer," notes from Course 1 at SIGGRAPH 94, "Animation Tricks," www.siggraph.org (March 3, 1999).

Chapter 7

1. Genesis 50:20

2. Luke 15

3. Luke 8:40–56

4. James 1:27

5. Kristen Anne Glover, "(Why) I Don't Want More Kids," www.fiveintow.com (December 20, 2014).

Chapter 8

1. Seth Godin, "The Problem with Hit Radio," www.sethgodin.typepad.com (May 28, 2014).

2. Saul McLeod, "Asch Experiment," www.simplypsychology.org (2008).

3. Daniel 1:17

4. Philippians 4:8

5. Follow this link to read my blog post and see pictures of that night at http://tomorrowsreflection.com/james-hetfield/, accessed July 7, 2015.

6. Romans 14:13–14

7. www.secondlife.com

Chapter 9

1. Acts 20:35

2. Gary Chapman, *The Five Love Languages* (Chicago: Northfield Publishing, 1992).

3. National Christian Foundation, "Alan Barnhart's Inspiring Business Gift" (May 20, 2013), http://www.nationalchristian.com/736, accessed July 7, 2015.

4. Tripp York and Justin Bronson Barringer, editors, *A Faith Not Worth Fighting For* (Eugene, OR: Wipf & Stock Publishers, 2012).

5. John 8:1–11

6. York and Barringer.

7. Ibid.

8. Ibid.

9. Ibid.

10. Luke 9:23b

11. Luke 9:24–25

12. Charles Dickens, *A Christmas Carol*, Chapter 5, emphasis added.

Chapter 10

1. Mike Brooks, Jeanne Meserve, and Mike Ahlers, "Airplane Crash-Lands into Hudson River; All Aboard Reported Safe," www.cnn.com (January 15, 2009).
2. Chip Heath and Dan Heath, *Decisive: How to Make Better Choices in Life and Work* (New York: Crown Business, 2013), 41.
3. See Greg Boyd's *God of the Possible* (Grand Rapids, MI: Baker Books, 2000) for an extensive study on the biblical examples of this concept.
4. 2 Kings 20:1
5. 2 Kings 20:5–6
6. Matthew 26:39–42
7. 1 Corinthians 13:12

Chapter 11

1. www.merriam-webster.com
2. "Baseball's Best Burger" described at www.gatewaygrizzlies.com/Famous_Food, accessed July 7, 2015.
3. Heinrich Heine, *Religion and Philosophy in Germany* (Albany: State University of New York Press, 1986), xi.
4. Austin Cline, "What Is Belief? What Does It Mean to Say 'I Believe' Something Is True?" http://atheism.about.com/od/definitionofatheism/a/BeliefImportant.htm, accessed July 7, 2015.
5. www.youversion.com
6. 2 Corinthians 5:17
7. Titus 2:11–12
8. 2 Peter 1:3–4
9. Matthew 20:1–16
10. "Saving Jeffrey Dahmer," http://www.beliefnet.com/Faiths/Christianity/2006/11/Saving-Jeffrey-Dahmer.aspx, accessed July 7, 2015.
11. Luke 15:11–32

ABOUT THE AUTHOR

JEREMY JERNIGAN serves as an executive pastor at Central Christian Church in the Phoenix area. He's a second-generation preacher with a passion for discovering and communicating truth. Jeremy has been married to Michelle for ten years, and they live in Arizona with their four kids. He's a voracious reader and has a borderline obsession for the Yankees (each of his kids have a middle name from a Yankee player).

Jeremy uses his blog, Tomorrow's Reflection, as his proving grounds for new ideas. Many of these ideas, and the feedback he receives on them, have grown into the content for his sermons and the book you are reading.

You can check out his blog at:
www.TomorrowsReflection.com

WORTHY®
PUBLISHING

If you enjoyed this book, will you consider sharing the message with others?

- Mention the book in a Facebook post, Twitter update, Pinterest pin, blog post, or upload a picture through Instagram.

- Head over to facebook.com/worthypublishing, "LIKE" the page, and post a comment as to what you enjoyed the most.

- Tweet "I recommend reading #RedeemingPleasure @JeremyJernigan // @worthypub"